NAMES OF NEW YORK

NAMES
OF NEW YORK

*Discovering the City's
Past, Present, and Future
Through Its Place-Names*

Joshua Jelly-Schapiro

Pantheon Books   *New York*

All rights reserved. Published in the United States by Pantheon Books,
a division of Penguin Random House LLC, New York, and distributed in
Canada by Penguin Random House Canada Limited, Toronto.

Pantheon Books and colophon are registered trademarks of
Penguin Random House LLC.

Library of Congress Cataloging-in-Publication Data

Name: Jelly-Schapiro, Joshua, author.
Title: Names of New York : discovering the city's past, present, and future
through its place-names / Joshua Jelly-Schapiro.
Description: New York : Pantheon Books, 2021. Includes index.
Identifiers: LCCN 2020037287 (print). LCCN 2020037288 (ebook).
ISBN 9781524748920 (hardcover). ISBN 9781524748937 (ebook)
Subjects: LCSH: Names, Geographical—New York (State)—New York.
New York (N.Y.)—Historical geography. New York (N.Y.)—History.
Classification: LCC F128.3 .J45 2021 (print) | LCC F128.3 (ebook) |
DDC 974.7/1—dc23
LC record available at lccn.loc.gov/2020037287
LC ebook record available at lccn.loc.gov/2020037288

www.pantheonbooks.com

Jacket image: *A Bird's Eye View of Lower Manhattan,* 1911,
by Richard Rummell. The New-York Historical Society, U.S.A./
Bridgeman Images
Jacket design by Jenny Carrow
Title page photo by Dario Lucarini from FreeImages

Printed in Canada
First Edition

2 4 6 8 9 7 5 3 1

For Mirissa

CONTENTS

NAMES OF NEW YORK

1.

THE POWER OF NAMES

Names matter. Just ask any parent agonizing over what to call a newborn. Or any kid burdened with a name they hate. Just think of the song made popular by Johnny Cash, about a boy who explains that "life ain't easy for a boy named Sue," and confronts the father who named him ("My name is Sue. How do you do! Now you gonna die!"). Whether you traverse your life as a Jane or an Ali or a Joaquin or an Eve—or you decide, as a grown-up, that you'd rather endure or enjoy it as someone else—we all learn that names mark us. Totems of identity, systems of allusion, names can signal where we're from, who our people are, who we attach ourselves to, which Bible character or dead relative or living movie star our namers loved best. Murmured by an intimate or yelled by a foe, a name can be an endearment or a curse. Declaimed by protesters in the street, a name becomes an assertion of dignity, of rights, and of the refusal to overlook or forget. Names are shorthand, they're synecdoche. They are acknowledgments or shapers of history, containers for memory or for hope. And if names matter so much when attached to people, they matter even more when attached to *places,* as labels that last longer, in our minds and on our maps, than any single human life.

"Name, though it seem but a superficial and outward matter, yet it carrieth much impression and enchantment." That's how Francis Bacon described the matrix of associations we affix, consciously or not, to the public words by which we navigate our days. Place-names can bind people together, or keep them apart. They can encode history and signal mores. They can proclaim what a culture venerates at one moment in time, and serve as vessels for how it evolves and shifts later on. Gettysburg, Attica, Stonewall, Rome. Wall Street, Main Street, Alabama, Prague. Malibu, Beirut, Boca Raton—place-names can summon worlds and evoke epochs in just a few syllables. They can recall long-ago events or become, as settings for more recent ones, metonyms for historical change. Place-names can become styles of dress (Bermuda shorts, Capri pants) and of dance (once we did the Charleston, now we do the Rockaway). They can hail rebellions or honor heroes or spring, like Sleepy Hollow and Zion, from books. Whether a name's born of whimsy or faith, whether it was first written down by a cavalier in his log or a bureaucrat in a city hall, its "impression and enchantment" derives, too, from the truth that its meaning can't be fully divorced from its roots.

In place-names lie stories. Stories, in the first instance, about their coiners—tales, say, about the long-ago Dutchmen who wandered an island of wetlands and hills that the people who lived there may or may not have called Mannahatta, but whose northern acreage those Dutchmen named for a marshy town in Holland called Haarlem. Then there are also stories about the complex or contradictory processes by which certain labels come to be recognized as "official." Stories about how people, singly or in groups, attach certain attributes to place-names that grow iconic (iconic of, for example, as with twentieth-century Harlem, Black culture and pride). And stories, too, about all the ways that such words thus do much more than merely label location. About how these words—in their rhythm and sound and how they look rendered into Roman letters or affixed on street signs and maps—shape our sense of place.

Toponymy—the study of place-names—isn't a well-known field. Say the term "toponymist" even to a professional geographer, and you'll conjure a hobbyist or word hoarder—a figure seen as a compiler of useful trivia. Some of us find our minds fed and our road trips improved by this kind of trivia, by learning, for example, that American place-makers fell in love with two sophisticated-sounding suffixes meaning "town," one borrowed from German (-burg) and one from French (-ville), with which they ran wild in naming Hattiesburg and Pittsburgh and Vicksburg and Fredericksburg and Charlottesville and

Hicksville and Danville (a village in Vermont near where I grew up, which one might incorrectly guess is named after a guy named Dan). We are intrigued to learn that during another bout of Francophilia, in the late 1800s, city planners who had wearied of the mundane word "street" began calling the broader ones by a term—"avenue"—which in France meant a tree-lined drive to a grand estate. Who, while walking down Manhattan's Mulberry Street, does not find the trip made richer by pondering how its blocks, long before they became home to Italian immigrants and then to the restaurants that still make its name synonymous with the best cannoli, were home until the 1850s to an actual mulberry tree? As legend, if not history, has it, the *Gangs of New York*–era folk hero Mose Humphrey pulled the tree up by its roots and used it to bludgeon rival toughs from the Plug Uglies.

Toponymy, at its simplest, is all about such bits of knowledge and lore. But as George R. Stewart, the doyen of American place-name lovers, observed, "the meaning of a name is bigger than the words composing it." And Marcel Proust agreed: In *Swann's Way,* he described how place-names "magnetized my desires" in his youth, "not as an inaccessible ideal but as a real and enveloping substance." The names that obsessed him weren't matched by the actual places; Parma was "compact, smooth," redolent of "Stendhalian sweetness and the reflected hue of violets," unlike the fusty and sprawling burgh in Northern Italy that he later visited. Proust was making a point similar to one that geographer Yi-Fu Tuan made in his book *Topophilia:* It's only in and through place—the places we love and leave and pass through and want to go to—that we figure out who we are. If language is consciousness and humans are a "place-loving species," then place-names—toponyms—may mold a larger piece of our minds than we think.

Place-names have the power not merely to locate experience, but to shape it: not merely to label the locales to which they refer but also "in some mysterious and beautiful way become part of [them]" as the writer Henry Porter put it. Portals through which to access the past, place-names are also a means to reexamine, especially in times of ire and tumult, what's possible. And nowhere is this more true than in a great city—a place, Tuan wrote, that "can be seen as a construction of words as much as stone." Cities are monuments to civilization, and its opposite. They're condensers of experience and creators of encounter. They're nothing if not generators of tales.

NEW YORK, THE CITY I know best, is in love with stories about itself. It's also not much occupied, in comparison with older towns across the sea, with its past. "Trees, a square, crooked old streets with Dutch or Flemish names. Few if any of us know the stories behind those names." So wrote Hilton Als, of his home and its habitués: "History takes too much time. We are Manhattanites and preoccupied by our lives in Manhattan." Luc Sante, another exemplary essayist of the city, agrees. "New York has no truck with the past," he wrote in *Low Life,* his great book about downtown before he got there. "It expels its dead." Sante meant this literally: To live in Manhattan is to see your remains carted off, once your life's exhausted, to a place whose cemeteries aren't already full. This is the city's centripetal force: its power to attract to itself the hungry who hope to make their own stories here and its sometimes-as-fierce will to cast them off.

The city has represented "an escape from the home-town and the homestead," Elizabeth Hardwick wrote— "an escape from the given." But to emerge from the subway onto Bleecker Street, as I do each morning on my way to work at NYU, is to step onto a byway that passes places whose names—Lafayette, Astor, Great Jones, Bond—beckon as signposts to illustrious or at least noto-rious New York figures of yore. (You're perhaps familiar with the names Astor and Lafayette, but Jones was an eighteenth-century politician whose namesake street got its "Great" to distinguish it from a shorter Jones Street nearby; much later, an alley adjacent to Great Jones Street that was frequented by junkies birthed the term "Jones-ing.") It is also to trace the route of what was once the edge of a homestead of Anthony Lispenard Bleecker, a banker whose farm in the 1700s lay a couple of miles north of New York City's edge. Of similar but even older prov-enance is the wider thoroughfare onto which I turn off

Bowery to reach my office: the Bowery (from the Dutch *bouwerij,* "farm road") led in the mid-1600s to the acreage of Peter Stuyvesant, New Netherlands' last Dutch governor, who counted among his peers Anthony Bleecker's great-granddad Jan, the first mayor of the Beaver District, upstate, that the Dutch named Beverwijck and we call Albany.

Few of the tattooed or besuited denizens of Bowery and Bleecker now, staring at their cellphones or heading home to obscenely priced flats or an NYU dorm, may know or care about these long-dead white men. But few who are invested in making their own New York stories on these blocks aren't mindful of denizens of more recent vintage. These names and images—from Basquiat to Blondie to Bob Dylan on the cover of *Freewheelin',* ambling along Bleecker with his girl—cling to these streets' names now, like chewing gum on pavement. And our sense that ghosts haunt these sidewalks, even if we can't know or perceive them at each turn, is vital to the larger meanings gained, over the last 350 years, by the city's name itself.

When in the summer of 1664 Richard Nicolls seized the Dutch port of New Amsterdam for the English, they weren't in the habit of naming their colonies "New" anything. It was thus with a perhaps wry nod to its Dutch founders that Nichols renamed the town for his patron in Britain. The place invoked by the Duke of York's title no doubt strikes many American ears, and English ones, too, as "just a name." But "York," like "Oxford" (where oxen forded a stream) or "Blackburn" (the brook there was dark-colored), is also a descriptive place-word. "York" derives from a Celtic word for "place of the yew tree," Eburāka, which passed through the mouths of successive invaders whose tongues reshaped it from Eboracum (Romans) to Eoforwic (Saxons) to Yorvik (Vikings) to York (English). Which is why and how when Frank Sinatra sang New York's name twice or Orphan Annie hailed "NYC!" or the rapper Nas parsed, in warier tones, his "New York state of mind," they were all hymning the allure and mental weather, whether they knew it or not, of the Duke's New Place of the Yew Tree.

To seek after place-names' roots in a young city of the New World, which counts its age not in millennia but in centuries, is usually easier than doing so in or near the ancient towns of Eurasia or Africa or the Levant— sites where the toponymist's art can involve a good deal of guesswork and daunting quests of philological detection into bygone people and tongues. This fact has long been vital to American scholars of place-names, and is the reason that George R. Stewart exulted, in *Names on the Land,* his bible of American toponymy, that the stories behind American names—from Cape Fear to Providence to Troublesome Creek—"were closely bound with the land itself and the adventures of the people." In 1945, he wrote that "In older countries the story of naming was lost in the ancient darkness. But in the land between the two oceans much of the record could still be read—who gave the names and when, and even why one name was chosen rather than another." Stewart penned *Names on the Land* during a war that saw not a few Germantowns and Hamburgs removed from Americans' maps and the name of their favorite form of processed meat changed—lest they be put in mind of the Führer when barbecuing on the Fourth of July—from frankfurters to hot dogs. Stewart's love for American names contains more than a hint of American jingoism (and an outmoded lack of discomfort with settler colonialism). But he was of course correct that maps of American cities are different beasts from those of Timbuktu or Berlin.

There are other reasons, which New York shares with other big cities, that pondering place-names here differs from pondering them in just any place. One of these is the outsized way that addresses here can connote prestige: There's a reason that Donald Trump, after acquiring what's now Trump International Tower by Columbus Circle, petitioned the city to make its official address One Central Park West (and then invested in a banner, facing a rival hotel across the way, to tout his petition's success). Another is the way that other names here, ones less evocative of global prestige than local pride, can travel. I wasn't alone, among members of my generation who grew up far from Queens, in nodding along to A Tribe Called Quest's ode to their home blocks' arboreal tag ("Linden Boulevard represent, repre-sent, -sent"). A metropolis is an object of desire and megaphone of culture: It produces more than its fair share of the cultural texts—TV shows and novels, pop songs and films—that we term "popular." Cities broadcast the names that comprise them outward.

Broadway is more than a road that traces an Indian trail whose width impressed the English; it's an adjective and a noun and an idiom of musical theater. When Manhattan's name is preceded by an indefinite article, it's also a bourbon-based cocktail first concocted at a tavern by the East River in Queens, whose barkeep's creation eased his patrons' waits for the ferry to its namesake. As Brooklyn has evolved, over recent decades, from a haven for immigrants to a gentrified home for the self-consciously hip, its moniker (which in Dutch meant "broken land") has become a mainstay in the Social Security Administration's list of Americans' fifty most popular names for baby girls. Of course such outward resonance isn't shared by every name or numbered street in its boroughs. Some streets' names are monumental only to their residents. But one distinctive feature of place-names in the city is the speed and force with which a label like "Lower East Side"—which once signified a German enclave and then a Jewish one before its newer denizens, from Puerto Rico, began calling it by a new tag, "Loisaida," that's now fastened to light poles on Avenue C—can see its connotations and even pronunciations change, across time, as its namesake blocks become home to new New Yorkers.

Much of our best recent writing about how "wisdom sits in places," as the Western Apache say, centers on landscapes we think of as "natural"—on the necessarily local or at least regional words, evolved by particular people in particular places, to describe the ecology where they live. The American writers Barry Lopez and Debra Gwartney, in a marvelous volume of American "landscape words" called *Home Ground,* collected terms ranging from "malpais" (as Arizonans call desert that's "cracked and reddish black like a pan of dried blood") to "cowbelly" (the fine silt beneath where an Appalachian stream runs calmest that's "soft as a Holstein's belly"). The British writer Robert Macfarlane's *Landmarks,* written in a similar vein, focused on the old tongues and dialects of the British Isles: His book includes poetic and suggestive terms for geographic and climatic features ranging from small bucket-sized islands in a bog (which folks in Exmoor call "zugs") to "the fine silver ice that coats all foliage when a freeze follows a thaw" (known in Devon as "ammil"). Macfarlane showed how, in an era of both linguistic homogenization and growing alienation from nature, such words can reenchant our "language for landscape," and, as Ralph Waldo Emerson put it, "fasten words again to visible things."

These books have much to teach about the power of language to vivify context and bind us to place. But to explore place-names in a city rather than a landscape that's natural or wild is to focus less on linguistic conservation than the notably urban form of linguistic evolution whereby a place-name that evoked one set of images or ideas a decade or a century ago may now evoke, and help create, a different place today. When some decades ago the storied *New Yorker* writer and fabulist Joseph Mitchell wanted a bracing whiff of the "Old New York" he loved, he headed to the piers that still lined Manhattan's chin like whiskers. "Seeking to rid my mind of thoughts of death and doom," he wrote, "I get up early and go down to Fulton Fish Market." He liked to breakfast there on shad-roe omelets at Sloppy Louie's, a place whose Genoese proprietor's fear of venturing to the upper stories of his old brick building, its rooms filled with naught but cobwebs and ghosts, furnished a classic meditation on Old New York's scent in its present. Now that the city's main fish market has moved up to Hunts Point in the Bronx, the old buildings where Fulton Street hits the East River are a tourist trap. With their landmarked façades sheltering purveyors not of herring or fluke but Dunkin' Donuts and GUESS jeans, they contain no floors their owners haven't leased. Walking there at dawn may not banish your deathly thoughts, unless sipping Dunkin' coffee on deserted cobbles named for Robert Fulton, inventor of steamships, floats your boat. But Mitchell's sense of the city's places and their people, as solace and as balm, is one shared by many writers of New York—from Alfred Kazin to Vivian Gornick and Paule Marshall and Ian

Frazier and Teju Cole—whose excavations of its crannies have nurtured mine.

Today the city's margins that are its lifeblood—the places where its past is most palpable, and where new immigrants shape its present—often lie beyond Manhattan. Sloppy Louie's proprietor was Genoese; new arrivals to the Bronx and Queens and Brooklyn's southern half now hail from Oaxaca and Haiti and Mali and Nepal. And on bright weekend mornings and gloomy Tuesday afternoons I've long made it my avocation, with the subway system that remains both the city's gift to explorers and what makes its culture go, to pore over maps of its boroughs and, like the narrator of Conrad's *Heart of Darkness* in his youth, to point to place-names that intrigue me—from Brooklyn's Dead Horse Bay, to Linoleumville and Victory Boulevard in Staten Island, to Featherbed Lane in the Bronx—with the idea: I will go there.

Digging into such toponyms' tales is its own reward. But that reward is made richer still for the lover of the city's juxtapositions and layers and rhymes who pays a visit to the places on the map in person. Take, for instance, Steinway Street in northwest Queens. Named for the German piano maker who in the 1870s opened a factory here that is still turning out the world's finest baby grands, Steinway is also now the name of the main drag in New York's Little Egypt. I have no idea what Mitchell's shad-roe omelet tasted like. But the thick Cairo-style coffee and pistachio halvah at El Khayam Cafe dished up by its charming proprietor, Gamal, to gringos and to regulars joshing in tuneful Arabic alike, is a breakfast—and a vision of New York now—that doom can't touch.

AS I AM A WRITER WHO is also a geographer, words and places duke it out daily for my mind's affections; it's hard to overstate the inbuilt joy to be won from such ventures where my two obsessions intersect, or from absorbing literature on the names that make up New York. In the frenetic span of history during which this once-colonial port grew to become the biggest city in its hemisphere (Gotham surpassed Mexico City in the 1830s), and then hurdled over London a century after that to become the most populous on earth, the city's place-names multiplied as fast as its populace—and saw some of its residents become their devoted students. The first of these was John J. Post; he published his three-volume *Old Streets, Roads, Lanes, Piers and Wharves of New York* in 1882. His intellectual heir Isaac Newton Phelps Stokes, whose hefty moniker perhaps fed his will not to be outdone, filled no fewer than six volumes with his encyclopedic *The Iconography of Manhattan Island,* released between 1915 and 1928. Over the decades since, these yeoman researchers have been joined by heirs whose labors' fruits are findable on the Internet and in tomes published by its boroughs' historical societies and others. It is to them that we owe the educated guesses that the Bronx's Featherbed Lane was named for bordellos on it once frequented by workers building the Croton Aqueduct, and that the names of the "fruit streets" of Brooklyn Heights—Cranberry, Pineapple, Orange—are owed either to a prosperous pair of local fruit merchants who named them as a marketing ploy or to a mischievous neighbor called Lady Middagh, who thought the area had too many streets named for wealthy families like hers and, in an act of DIY urbanism avant la lettre, tacked up fruit-themed signs instead (she left Middagh Street alone).

But to ponder place-names today requires considering questions not merely of origins but of power. It means asking who has the power to name and why—to question why the powers that be, or were, saw fit to make those fruit streets a part of Brooklyn's map. It also crucially means, in this era of pulling down statues and reckoning with our collective past, engaging questions around when and why we should change street names that honor, say, historical figures whose business wasn't selling oranges but people. New York was a slave port just like Charleston and New Orleans, though it has long pretended otherwise, and no fewer than seventy streets in Brooklyn alone, by one count, are still named for slave owners. Calls to remove names of people who weren't merely of their time but backed its evils with arms—Brooklyn's Fort Hamilton still has byways named for Robert E. Lee and Stonewall Jackson—have been joined by a surge of new and honorary street names hailing historic antiracists from Toussaint L'ouverture to Shirley Chisholm and Malcolm X.

A similar conversation is ongoing with regard to streets and monuments—as with the recently removed statue of Theodore Roosevelt that depicts the Rough Rider lording it over African and Amerindian attendants outside the Museum of Natural History—that glorify the colonial enterprise that began in the Americas in 1492. That enterprise also birthed the trading post that became New York, before overspreading a continent whose decimated first people saw their languages' singing consonants become key to American place-names in a manner whose basal dynamic is distilled in an episode that occurred not in these parts, but out west.

It involves the first white men to enter the sublime valley in California's Sierra Nevada that became the United States' foremost "natural cathedral" and first national park. When in 1851 the Army captain Lafayette Bunnell scrambled into the Yosemite Valley and his men claimed its waterfalls for their gold-miner friends, they encountered a band of the area's native people, whose surrender their guns quickly won. Bunnell explained to those Northern Miwoks' defeated leader, Tenaya, that his people would now be brought from where they'd gathered acorns under misty peaks for millennia to a reservation in California's sunbaked Central Valley. By the stone-rimmed edge of a high lake that the Miwok called Pyweack, or "shining rocks," Bunnell told Tenaya to cheer up: He'd chosen, he said, to name its clear waters Lake Tenaya, "because it was upon the shores of the lake that we had found his people, who would never return to it to live." Bunnell ignored Tenaya's protest that the lake already had a name, but did register, in his memoir of their encounter, the Indian's downcast face. "His countenance indicated that he thought the naming of the lake no equivalent for his loss of territory."

What's notable about this episode, as Rebecca Solnit wrote in her haunting account of it, was how it collapsed two stages of historical change—a culture's annihilation and its romanticization—into a single meeting: an exchange that made plain to Tenaya not merely that he now had no place in his ancestral home's present, but that his name was going to be used there to adorn someone else's future. It's also striking for how it captures several of the things—from describing nature that is present to monumentalizing people who aren't—that names can do. Today's picnickers quaffing Cokes by Lake Tenaya may not be put in mind, by its name, of the Miwok chief or of dispossession. But surfacing such pasts—and showing the power of names to do so—suffuses Solnit's *Savage Dreams,* a book that anyone interested in California and landscape and politics must read. It's also suffused my work with Solnit, in the years since we became collaborators and decided to do a project about the city where I live, and where the stories of both my forebears and Rebecca's, like those of many Americans, run through Ellis Island.

That book, *Nonstop Metropolis,* was an atlas of New York based on the idea that any city contains at least as many ways to be mapped as it does people. Its subjects ranged from the eight hundred languages now spoken in Queens to the fires that ravaged the Bronx in the 1970s, and aimed to suggest how maps of such themes can help us see the city in new ways. To research and create them was to grow immersed in the names that are the basic building blocks of any map, and to become fascinated by how people use those names drawn from many tongues, or craft new ones in their own, to "make place" in the city. It was also to grow convinced of the truth, whether your daily commute involves hopping the C train at Hoyt-Schermerhorn or taking a ferry to Red Hook, that your sense of wonder can be deepened only by learning that the Schermerhorns of Brooklyn were a family of ship-chandlers whose namesake street gained its moniker from their employees' custom of using its length as a "rope-walk" for braiding lengths of cord; or that the choppy stretch of water you cross from Wall Street to reach Red Hook's Atlantic Basin, the Buttermilk Channel, may have won its name from long-ago Brooklyn dairy farmers, who imagined the milk they floated to market might be churned to butter by its waves.

This book grew from that conviction, and from a

happy autumn when I had the fortune to ride that ferry to Red Hook a few times a week. It was in an old ironworks there, on a street named Pioneer, between two others named Coffey and Van Brunt, in a brick building that now houses not machines but art, that it got under way. Whatever streets you're near or places you hold dear, my hope is that this book might perhaps help you see their names—and what they do—anew.

2.

THE NAMES BEFORE

What's more American than naming stuff for people you've killed? Not much, to judge from a nation where no fewer than twenty-six states—along with thousands of towns, countless sports teams, and innumerable summer camps and recreational vehicles—bear names meant to evoke those humans who came before: the indigenous, whose speech suggested alluring ties to a wild landscape whose settling, for its colonizers, required those peoples' removal. Between 1492 and the American Revolution, this continent's indigenous populace declined from an estimated ten million people to a tenth of that. This slow genocide had many effects. Among the less-discussed is linguistic: millions of words, in thousands of dialects and tongues, that evolved over millennia. Perhaps a quarter of the earth's languages in the fifteenth century, linguists say, were North American. Lost to us now are countless words that described the grasslands and gullies and oxbows and peaks of the lands these varied peoples inhabited and shaped. But not a few of their proper names and place-words, or misconstruals thereof, were placed on old maps and remain on ours.

When it comes to memorialization, nothing beats a martyr—even when your culture has done the martyring. Nothing beats a figure who's fixed in time and unsullied by its passing for projecting ideals onto. Any teenager who's hung up a poster of a rock star or revolutionary who died young can tell you that. Which is part of why the original long-haired rebels in American culture have been a popular source for American toponyms since the late summer's day, in 1609, when Henry Hudson angled his ship through an inviting narrows and entered an expansive bay. Hudson crossed that bay and began sailing up the broad river that would later be named for him. As he did, a group of Indians they met, according to the journal of one of Hudson's seamen, pointed to the wooded land to starboard and said: "Mannahatta."

The first word of those Native Americans' language to be adopted by Europeans became its most famous—and the first of many whose meaning no European properly learned (or wrote down, in any case). The people Hudson met there, who spoke an Algonquian tongue called Munsee, had beat him to Mannahatta by a thousand years or so. Their forebears had left the Eurasian landmass some millennia earlier. After striding west over the Bering land bridge, they gradually traversed the continent, across generations and centuries, to find their lasting home by its fecund eastern edge, in the acorn- and deer-filled woods surrounding a sublime natural bay whose depths teemed with fish and whose shallows breathed with a billion oysters. They inhabited an archipelago of clan-based villages set in woodland clearings and by the streams and marshlands of an ancestral homeland that stretched between what's now Trenton and where the Hudson, at Storm King, descends seaward from the Catskills.

In colonial days, these people and their southerly cousins, who spoke a related but distinct Algonquian tongue called Unami, both came to be called Delawares. The label came from the same English noble—Thomas West of Wherwell, the 3rd Baron De La Warr—whose name the English also stuck to a big river and the small colony by its mouth that later became a small state. Nowadays, descendants of those "Delawares" refer to themselves by their ancestors' shared word—Lenape—for human being. The fact that we don't know exactly why the Lenape who met Hudson's boat called the river's eastern shore Manahata is related to another fact: that the virtues of their home harbor as an anchorage, which Hudson claimed for his sponsor (stockholders in the Dutch East India Company), were as plain as the riches to be had from turning the area's beavers and foxes into "skins and peltries . . . and other commodities." Within a century and a half of Hudson's arrival, most of the Lenape were either dead or dispersed to begin their long journey, by way of proximate forests and tribes, toward reservations in Ontario and Oklahoma, where their scant descendants now live.

In those Munsee speakers' absence, it was for many years left to non-native philologists to offer theories about the etymology of "Manhattan." For much of the nineteenth century, the most accepted version seemed to be one offered by a scholar named John Gottlieb Ernestus Heckewelder at the 1822 meeting of the American Philosophical Society. Heckewelder, who was faulted by subsequent linguists for associating rather too many Lenape words with drinking alcohol, proposed that Mannahatta was actually a misrendering of Manahachtanienk—"island where we all became intoxicated." The more sober translation you may have learned in school is "island of hills." This translation is owed to Heckewelder's scholarly heir, William Wallace Tooker, who published his muchcited article "The Origin of the Name Manhattan" in 1901. In recent decades, fresh research by linguists and native activists given to consulting native culture bearers and the Lenape descendants themselves has yielded different theories. The most widely credited comes from a fluent Munsee speaker and scholar in Canada named Albert Anthony, who died a long time ago but who explained before he did that *man-a-ha-tonh* meant "place where we gather timber for bows and arrows."

Whether or not those were the syllables that Hudson's sailor heard (and other modern scholars argue he may have simply heard *menating*—"island") we'll never know.

But the island they described did indeed have stands of hard hickory and ash that were good for crafting weapons from. And in 1626, as the famous story would have it, some Dutch traders convinced the Indians who lived there to part with what would become the world's most valuable island for pocket change. That tale, and our recollection of the negotiation at its heart, required a native-sounding place-name to work. Manhattan would do, and has.

FEW OBSESSIONS SO EXERCISE modern New Yorkers like real estate regret ("If only I'd bought in 1983!"), and what the city's most infamous real estate huckster turned American president termed "the Art of the Deal." This, one suspects, is why no morsel of early New York history is better known by modern New Yorkers than the tale of Manhattan's acquisition—albeit in a version suffused with hyperbole and misinformation of the sort that wheeler-dealers like Donald Trump, when acquiring the same island's real estate later on, made their stock-in-trade.

In 1626, the Dutchman Peter Minuit was doing the same thing when he gave the Lenape "sixty Guilders worth of goods" to allow the Dutch to inhabit and build homes on Manhattan. His deal to do so may have struck him as a good bargain. But it certainly wasn't as advantageous as you'd be led to believe by tour guides and easy-chair historians who cite the sum that Minuit is said to have spent—twenty-four dollars—without noting that this meaningless number comes from a nineteenth-century historian's rough calculation as to what sixty Dutch guilders equaled in U.S. currency in 1846. And the Lenape who accepted Minuit's proposal and gifts didn't think they were getting a raw deal—and not merely because the ones with whom Minuit dealt may in fact have been a band of Canarsees who didn't live in Manhattan at all, and were thus extra-pleased to return to their home village, on the other end of what's now Brooklyn, with a haul of new axes and Jew's harps and iron pots. In their culture, property rights were determined not by deed but by a practice similar to our legal concept of usufruct: the right of a person or clan, so long as they were making productive use of a patch of earth, to continue doing so. Whichever band of Lenape it was that Minuit dealt with, their giving his people leave to make use of Manhattan wouldn't have struck them as an arrangement in perpetuity—and didn't. Dutch colonial records are full of references to a continued Lenape presence on this island whose new "owners" were induced by their neighbors, for many years after Minuit gave up those sixty guilders of goods, to furnish further tribute.

For most early Dutch settlers who wanted, on the one hand, to be allowed to sleep safely at night in their vulnerable homes and, on the other, to obtain furs to fill ships bound for Amsterdam, befriending their Indian neighbors was a wiser tack than antagonizing them. For a few years in the 1640s, an ill-tempered chief of their colony, Willem Kieft, sought—with disastrous results that saw him relieved of his post—to erase Indians from New Netherlands' map. But in general, the decades during which the Dutch held their colony, and those immediately following the English takeover of it in 1664, were defined less by war than by trade. Most trade was conducted with strands of cylindrical shell beads that the Lenape called "sewant" and white men called "wampum," between parties who communicated in a Munsee-Dutch trade pidgin that was until as recently as the 1970s still spoken by descendants of the Ramapo band of Lenape in northern New Jersey. (You'd be forgiven for thinking that the sundry creole tongues of America's colonial age survive only in the Caribbean, but until a few decades ago, all you had to do was head across the George Washington Bridge and drive for about twenty miles toward the wooded uplands where five thousand current members of the Ramapough Lenape Indian Nation share a tribal name—Ramapo means "under the rock"—with the mountains where they live.)

In the faster-moving later chapters of American settler colonialism, manifest destiny's march to the Pacific meant constant war and transfer of land from native peoples to whites, under a pall of fated extermination, by deceit or theft or both. But over the first century of European Indian cohabitation in what became greater New York, the means by which Dutch and Englishmen acquired Lenape land was signing purchase agreements with people who grew familiar with what was meant by transferring a deed, and practiced at playing colonists and buyers off each other to gain a better price. Like indigenous people across the hemisphere, many bands of Lenape were decimated by Old World germs. But some also managed, in their weakened state, to sell off their lands piece by piece before finally deciding to pull up stakes, at a time and for a price of their liking, and move inland or upriver to let these white people do what they wished with their foothold on this vast continent's edge.

Within a few decades of New Amsterdam becoming New York in 1664, and especially after the signing of the 1758 Treaty of Easton, which aimed to push all the area's Indians west of the Alleghenies, holdouts like the Ramapo were more exception than rule. The sheer force of numbers and germs, as successive waves of colonists arrived with their sheep and pigs and the pathogens they'd acquired from living in close quarters with both, succeeded in pushing all but a few Lenape (along with the Esopus and Wappingers and Mahicans from up the Hudson Valley) from their ancestral homes. But before they left, various of their names and words came to grace the old colony's hinterlands: that perimeter of hills and fields within a hundred miles of Manhattan whose old Indian-ish names now belong to the bedroom communities of the commuteriat served by Metro-North and the Long Island Rail Road.

Some of the labels that showed up then on maps and remain on ours belonged to sachems who haggled over prices and acreage and left their mark on colonial deeds (Katonah, Kensico). Others use Munsee words whose origins as place-names (Armonk means "place of dogs"; Ho-Ho-Kus means "little bottle gourd") remain obscure. It was in the 1890s that elegant denizens of the Tuxedo Park Club, in the tony town of that name in Orange County, cut the tails of their English-style dinner jackets to make the dark suits still worn by prom- and wedding-goers now. But centuries before they did so, the Munsee word "ptukwsiituw" referred to members of their Wolf Clan (and derived from their word for "round foot") who lived there. The name of Ossining, in Westchester County, may now put one in mind of John Cheever's adulterous fictions or of Sing Sing prison; once, it was a Munsee word for "stony place." On Long Island, several town names borrowed from local bands of Lenape (Massapequa, Matinecock) or the Pequot-speaking peoples, farther east, whose kinship ties reached across the water to Connecticut and whose names (Manhasset, Montauket) now adorn golf courses and swish resorts where city folk use the word "summer" as a verb. At least the Shinnecock won federal tribal recognition in 2010. Now they've got their own piece of the Hamptons, and a permanent reservation there, to live on or monetize as they wish.

·   ·   ·

BACK BY NEW YORK HARBOR and in the old Lenape homeland on the Hudson's western bank, many lasting place-names express the aqueous character of an estuarine world. In the marshes-and-malls landscape of what's now the Meadowlands, not a few native place-words—Passaic ("river flowing through a valley"); Hackensack (from the Munsee "achkincheschakey": "stream which discharges itself into another on the level ground"); Raritan ("point in a tidal river")—were also bands of people. The home zone of the Raritans, in the early 1600s, included a large island whose cultural and geographic ties, then as now, joined it more closely to New Jersey than to New York. After a Raritan sachem named Pierwim signed over Staten Island's last unbought parcel to the English in 1670, their name for what later became New York's fifth borough—Aquehonga Manacknong: "place of the bad woods"—didn't stick. Whether this was because of its cumbersome length or its foreboding vibe, the word "Raritan" itself fared better: It still names New Jersey's longest river and the bay it drains into. Our modern moniker for the town overlooking both, Perth Amboy, is a portmanteau of the Scottish city for which Perth, Australia, is also named, and a liberal transcription of the Lenape word "ompoge," for "level place."

In the Bronx, "Mosholu" was perhaps a Munsee term for a stream the English redubbed Tibbetts Brook but whose burbling syllables, meaning "smooth stones," now name a traffic-clogged parkway. Gowanus, to modern-day Brooklynites, may be a polluted canal. But once it was a life-giving stream whose Munsee name the Dutch perhaps adopted because of its resemblance to that of Holland's Gouwe River. Maspeth, across another dirty waterway between Brooklyn and Queens, now calls to mind Polish neighbors and warehouses. To its coiners, who by some sixth sense seem to have foreseen the future Superfund status of Newtown Creek, its name meant "bad water" (which made Maspeth a kind of obverse to Amagansett, whose name meant "good water" to the Montauketts of eastern Long Island). Across Queens and around the marshy world of islands and grasses abutting JFK Airport, a spate of Munsee names—Rockaway (from "leekuwahkuy," meaning "sandy place"); Hassock ("marshy"); Neponsit ("place between the waters")—describe the squishy reed-lands ringing Jamaica Bay. So does that of nearby Canarsie, which, centuries before it became known as the L train's Brooklyn terminus, was the site of a Lenape village whose name perhaps meant "high grasses."

The moniker of Jamaica Bay itself, which it shares with both Jamaica, Queens, and a Caribbean island known for reggae music and Red Stripe beer, was also long said to have Lenape roots. But recently this theory was debunked by the leading scholar of New York's native place-names. Robert Grumet noted that the sole evidence for etymologists' old claim that "Jamaica" is a misspelling of a lost Munsee word is a colonial document, from 1656, stating an English farmer's purchase of an area "near unto the Beaver Pond commonly called Jemaico." Grumet has proposed instead that the English got their name for this part of Queens from the same source that inspired that of Boston's Jamaica Plain: a certain sugar island in the West Indies that was, in the seventeenth and eighteenth centuries, the British empire's most lucrative possession. By what mystic force the Jamaica in New York, out by JFK Airport and along the Long Island Rail Road route to Babylon, has in recent decades also become home to many immigrants from the Jamaica in the Caribbean, is hard to say. But the name of those immigrants' Caribbean homeland is an indigenous word, too: it means, in the language of Arawak people who lived there once, "land of wood and water."

When Columbus bumped into that island and several others nearby, the Caribbean was inhabited by Arawak and Taíno people from whose language not a few other words—especially around the time of year of our Puerto Rican Day Parade ("Boricua!")—are heard in the lived lingo of New York's streets. But the European conception of the New World as virgin land was never in conflict with their habit of adorning its features with verbal reminders of its natives—whether with an authentic or an authentic-sounding word, if one was at hand, or a generic one if one wasn't. Such are the roots, across America, of scores of Indian Rivers and Indian Creeks and Indian Fields that gained their names not because of known associations with bygone tribes but in a manner similar to how the Indian Lake in the Bronx, an algae-clogged bowl in Crotona Park, won its moniker. "Local boys," explains the borough's toponymist-in-chief, John McNamara, "gave the lake its name."

THERE'S AN IMPLICIT CHALLENGE for hobbyists and scholars seeking to work backward from written "Indian words" which are in fact only transliterated renderings, often flawed, of Munsee or Chippewa or Mahican speech as it struck the ears of Dutch- or English- or Frenchmen in Roman letters. This challenge is why even leading experts in the continent's first tongues often disagree about place-names' meanings (and why those I'm citing here are in many cases no better than those experts' best guesses). Early on, not a few places in New York's larger region got names whose provenance is clear. Connecticut is one Frenchman's respectable attempt at writing down the word the Mohegan people used for the broad river, flowing south from Quebec to the Long Island Sound, that in their language perhaps sounded more like "quinetucket" ("beside the long, tidal river"). But later on and out west, many coiners of ever-proliferating new place-names and states' names seem to have embraced Indian names less as a means of tapping into an authentic expression of place than as a shorthand way to invoke a certain wild beauty. When in 1868 the namers of the Wyoming

Territory were brainstorming worthy names for that vast tract of high plains and peaks, they were inspired by Thomas Campbell's popular poem "Gertrude of Wyoming." It recalled a woman from the Wyoming Valley in Pennsylvania, whose name to its Lenape coiners meant "a flat place." But at least "Wyoming" was an actual word in an actual native tongue. Idaho, coined in the 1860s by a frontiersman-huckster who claimed to speak Shoshone but plainly didn't, just sounded like one.

But sound matters to romantics. Especially to that breed of romantic whose great love is America. It certainly did to New York's best-known such figure. Walt Whitman was, naturally, a great lover of Indian names. He explained why in his *An American Primer.* "I was asking for something savage and luxuriant," wrote the poet, "and behold here are the aboriginal names. They all fit!" He offered the ready example: "Mississippi!—the word winds with chutes—it rolls a stream three thousand miles long." Whitman didn't note, in doing so, that the phrase "Mississippi River" is redundant: combining the Anishinaabe Algonquian term for "great river" and the English generic, it means "great river river." The name of the Ohio River (Ohio is Iroquois for "great river") denotes the same thing. Such infelicities are perhaps inevitable when combining two tongues in geographic ways. But sometimes such combos work out nicely indeed. They did in the case of New York's euphonious Tappan Zee—a Dutch-era name for where the Hudson widens to a lake-like breadth north by Tarrytown, that combines the name of a Lenape tribe who lived there and the Dutch word for "sea."

In the decades leading up to and following the United States' Declaration of Independence, many of the ex-Englishmen who became founding fathers, and settlers who carved new homesteads and villages from the Northeast's forests, embraced a fashion for naming their new outposts of civilization for old Greek ones—Syracuse, Ithaca, Utica, Troy. Upstate New York also filled with foreign-sounding nations and towns—Cuba, Cairo, Sweden, Peru—whose names they also liked. But over the span of American life that corresponded with Whitman's own—years stretching from the forced removal of the East's last tribes along the Trail of Tears, to those years after the Civil War when railways and telegraph poles overspread the continent and the Postal Service added forty thousand station names to its directory—many people seemed to agree with Whitman that its first nations' "savage and luxuriant" syllables well fit its landscape. In that era, a hugely popular newspaper column, "Letters from Podunk," made that Algonquian place-word synonymous with out-of-the-way. By now, Americans also had a pantheon of famed native chiefs whose courage in defending their people was perhaps easier to admire in defeat. Many of those leaders' names—Pontiac, Tecumseh, Seattle—became towns and cities, too. Osceola, the famous Seminole warrior, may have lived in Florida and died there in 1838, but his name was stuck to no fewer than seventeen far-flung places, in the decades after he died, all across the land.

In America's biggest city, this trend wasn't so pronounced as it was in the counties in New Jersey and Pennsylvania where people named new towns after the hero of *The Song of Hiawatha,* Henry Wadsworth Longfellow's hugely popular 1855 poem about a noble Indian who shared his name with a storied Iroquois statesman. By then, New York City was old by American standards. Its powers-that-be weren't as open as those in other districts to being renamed for Native Americans either made up or real. But this wasn't for lack of trying, in the late nineteenth century, by romantic revivalists. One such was Henry Rowe Schoolcraft, an enterprising ethnologist who during a stint working for the Indian Bureau in Minnesota married an Ojibwe woman from whose Algonquian tongue Schoolcraft sought, once the pair settled in New York, to craft place-names suggestive of their lost Lenape ones. A few of the names he propagated in this way— Ellis Island became Kioshk ("gull island"), Brooklyn Heights became Ihepatonga ("high sandy banks")—grew briefly popular, before expiring. More lasting was the respected Bronx historian Thomas H. Edsall's proposal, in the 1890s, to rename a hill by his home in Riverdale for a native word he thought apt. No Lenape ever referred to that place by the Algonquian word Edsall riffed on to name it Shorackappock, or "sitting-down place at a high height." But you'll find the place where he did if, while trundling down the Henry Hudson Parkway toward Spuyten Duyvil, you keep an eye out, after passing the exit for 232nd Street, for the one marked Kappock Street.

THAT SAME BOROUGH'S Cayuga Avenue was named, depending on which account you read, either by local residents who thought Van Cortlandt Lake resembled Cayuga Lake near Ithaca or by a Cornell University–educated surveyor with fond memories of swimming there. Less mysterious in origin is another Indian word from across the Empire State that motorists on the West Side Highway long ago grew used to glimpsing across the river, painted in capital letters on the side of a building in Hoboken (whose own name likely derives from "hopoakan," "tobacco pipe"). That word painted on the terminal's back side—Lackawanna—labels the old eastern terminus of the Delaware, Lackawanna, and Western Railroad, which from 1853 to 1960 brought anthracite coal to the Hudson's edge from the steel town by Lake Erie whose fun-to-say name has inspired blues songs and TV shows but whose syllables actually meant "forked river" in Unami. Lackawanna, beyond being that town's name, is also a river in Pennsylvania that flows past Scranton and into the Susquehanna (the "oyster river," whose name must derive from the once-mighty colony of bivalves where it hits the Chesapeake). More proximate among

Indian words familiar to denizens of Manhattan's West Side is little Weehawken Street in the Village: Its tag is owed to people who came there for market, in olden days, from the cliffside town across the river (whose name, in Munsee, means "by the big land").

As the nineteenth century became the twentieth, and such vernacular sources for New York places were increasingly supplanted by names born not of local history but of developers' schemes, the part of the northern Bronx once known as Woodmansten but renamed Morris Park around 1900 acquired a Seminole Avenue, a Choctaw Place, and a Pawnee Place, too. Nearby Narragansett Avenue wasn't named for Rhode Island's first peoples or the cheap beer now hawked with their name; it's owed to a developer who thought it would be nice to name streets here, in an area he called Westchester Heights, for summer resorts (others nearby included Saratoga and Newport) in order to put residents in mind, even as they trudged over February's icy pavements, of a holiday. It's not likely that the builders of the Montauk Club in Brooklyn had something similar in mind, in 1889, when they erected that Gilded Age pile that's modeled on a palazzo in Venice. But it's a fair bet that the name of Park Slope's most popular wedding venue now reminds guests less of eastern Long Island's first peoples than of vacationing at one of the beach hotels now peopling their dunes.

Manhattan's Cherokee Place, off 77th Street on the Upper East Side, was named for a similar establishment called the Cherokee Club. That establishment (now the Cherokee Apartments) was opened in 1905 by members of Tammany Hall's Democratic machine: corrupt men who loved associating themselves with (their idea of) wild Indians but whose club's oak-paneled rooms, it feels safe to surmise, never welcomed an actual Cherokee (to say nothing of any actual kin of Tammany, the Lenape leader for whom they named their syndicate). Not all such borrowings from faraway native tongues, on the modern cityscape, have such corrupt roots. The leafy corner of Queens that's now Kissena Park is one such: It's a part of Flushing known for its cherry blossoms and weeping beeches, in a neighborhood whose storefronts' signage is now mostly in Chinese but whose own name is owed to the noted nineteenth-century botanist and landscape architect Samuel Bowne Parsons. The Parsons family's famous plant nursery was the source of American gardeners' flowering dogwoods and rhododendrons, but Parsons took the name for Kissena Lake, on what was his nursery's grounds before it became a city park, from an imported Ojibwe word for "it is cold."

The era when Parsons did so was the epoch of the Battle of the Little Bighorn, out west, and the "closing of the frontier": a period that saw many Americans grow perversely nostalgic for when Indian victories like Custer's last stand didn't yet register as the defiant death cry of a doomed race. As America's last wildernesses and their people were brought to heel after 1900, Edmund Curtis's stark black-and-white portraits of aged chiefs in pigtails circulated widely in the culture. A push to commemorate the vanquished went so far as to see Congress furnish land by New York's Narrows in Staten Island in 1911 for the purpose of building a National American Indian Memorial. The project was the brainchild of department store magnate Rodman Wanamaker, who wanted to build a 165-foot-tall statue of an Indian—taller than the Statue of Liberty—atop a museum on the site.

His plan advanced far enough to see President William Howard Taft, in 1913, travel to Fort Wandsworth and a site now shadowed by the Verrazzano Bridge, for a groundbreaking. But then World War I, and the discovery that Wanamaker didn't have funds for construction, doomed the scheme. This, given the gargantuan cigar store Indian at that scheme's heart, was perhaps for the best. But it does mean that the city's only official monuments, today, remain a pair of markers that commemorate not New York's first people but their "sale" of Manhattan to the Dutch. One of these stands by the Battery downtown. It was gifted to the city by the government of the Netherlands in 1926, and comprises a statue of Peter Minuit standing with what appears to be a caricature of a Sioux brave from the plains in a feathered headdress. The other is a plaque in Inwood Park, by the island's northern tip, near caves said to have once been used by the Lenape there. It claims that Minuit's capture of their island occurred here, at "the site of the principal

Manhattan Indian village," rather than a dozen miles to the south.

THESE MEMORIALS GET A lot baldly wrong. But what's most offensive about them is the way they're predicated on commemorating what Rodman Wanamaker, the department store magnate, dubbed a "vanishing race"—on placing America's first people wholly in its past. Which is an insult to all their descendants, who haven't vanished at all, but instead live modern lives shadowed by past violence. Even and especially in New York City, which may not be a place one much identifies with Amerindians now, but whose populace includes more of them—forty thousand, as of the last census—than any other U.S. city. This is not because, as in Tucson and Missoula and Juneau, native homelands linger nearby. New York's first peoples are in fact dispersed. It's just because this city has more of everyone—including members of tribal nations from across the continent—than anywhere else.

Nowadays, their presence is hailed loudly in annual powwows that bring Mohawk drummers and Aztec dancers and Abenaki elders to Inwood Park each July, and to Randall's Island in the East River each October, to sing songs and eat fry bread and urge New York City to start celebrating not Columbus Day but Indigenous Peoples' Day instead. But the Native American presence in New York also has to do with the ways Native Americans, when not donning traditional garb, but the uniforms of workaday life, have shaped the modern city. Many of that city's skyscrapers were built by the famous "Mohawks in High Steel" who, starting in the 1920s, traveled here from reservations upstate, bringing a collective immunity to vertigo that saw them become the go-to workers on the tallest buildings (and forge an enclave in the Gowanus section of Brooklyn). Those fearless Mohawks literally shaped the city. But so too has the city's culture been shaped, in ways more ephemeral but just as deep, by figures ranging from Maria Tallchief, the Oklahoma-born Osage who became America's first prima ballerina in the 1950s, to La India, the Bronx-reared Puerto Rican queen of Latin radio in a town where Latinos have ruled radio for decades, whose name hails the Taíno past of her native Borinquen. In recent years, new arrivals from still-indigenous sectors of this hemisphere—speakers of Aymara and Quechua from the Andes; of Mixtec and Mayan from Mexico; of Tzotzil and K'iche' from Guatemala—have come to fill vital roles in the city's economy and to ensure that many of its restaurant's kitchens, although filled with immigrants from Latin America, are places whose main language is not Spanish. And less visible but no less key, in recent years, has been the slow but steadily rising return to visibility—and to Manhattan—of its own first people.

Since 2008, the Lenape Center of Manhattan has maintained an active office, under the aegis of the New York Foundation for the Arts, in the core of what its directors call Lenapehoking: the Lenape homeland. None of those directors lives here: The center's cofounder, Curtis Zunigha, resides on Delaware Tribal land in Bartlesville, Oklahoma. But the center maintained an active role in what's become a burgeoning effort, especially at city universities, to get local academics and public agencies to add to their papers and policies the sort of "land acknowledgment statements" their peers have long had in Australia. In 2016, the son of a wealthy artist in the part of Manhattan the Lenape called Sapokanikan ("tobacco field") and that's now the West Village deeded a $4 million town house to the tribe. ("This building is the trophy from major theft," he explained. "It disgusts me.") On Staten Island, a part-Lenape woman named Margaret Boldeagle has won support from local officials in her quest to see old Rodman Wanamaker's monument finally erected, a century late and in different form, but with a more evolved grasp of how America's first peoples didn't die out after all. And on the third Friday of each month, in a windowless office near Union Square, the island's first tongue is stirring back to life.

Karen Hunter, the woman who leads Lenape classes there in the office of the Endangered Language Alliance, lives on the Delaware Nation reservation in Ontario. There, she's known as the foremost student of a language whose last known native speaker will die any day. On 18th Street in Manhattan, Karen and her husband idle in her Dodge minivan, if they've made good time on the twelve-hour drive down from Canada, to wait until street parking opens up at 6:00 p.m. And then Karen, a onetime Canadian weight-lifting champion with copper skin and smiling eyes, climbs the stairs to teach. Among her students, when I attended one recent evening, was an NYU student in Doc Martens who said she wanted to "decolonize my mind," and a gray-goateed man who said he'd spent his working life teaching Chinese medicine, but was devoting his retirement to leading the Turkey Clan of Matinecock in eastern Queens. Also present was Ross Perlin of the Endangered Language Alliance, a linguist who grew up amid New York's Yiddish speakers, but whose area of specialization, when he's not nurturing the endangered tongues of his hometown, is studying those of the Himalaya. Karen ran through some warm-up sounds we'd need to speak Lenape. All of us did our best. We did so again as she asked us to repeat after her. "Nii noonjiyayi Lenapehoking," she said. "I am from the Lenape homeland." Some of us, repeating after her, sounded better than others. "Nii noonjiyayi Lenapehoking." She smiled all the same.

3.

NAVIGATORS AND DUYVILS
AND ENGLISH AND KINGS
(ON COLONIAL NAMES)

For the past action-packed half-millennium of human history, naming places has been an activity closely allied to another oft-imperial enterprise: mapping. Since the so-called Age of Exploration, those who've arrogated to themselves the right to claim continents have also charted them. Before America was a place or even an idea, it was a word on a map: one coined in 1507 by Martin Waldsee-müller, a German cartographer who published Europe's first chart of a new landmass onto which he stuck a word derived from the given name of a sailor from Florence, Amerigo Vespucci, who'd recently skirted its coast from the Orinoco to Brazil. Vespucci saw his Latinate nick-name label a land that kings and trading companies across Europe were hiring Italian navigators like him to explore. Their hope was to find, as Columbus never did, a westward passage to China.

England's Henry VII got in on this act by turning to a seaman who was born Giovanni Caboto in Genoa, or maybe Zuan Chabotto in Venice, but who is in any case better known by his Anglo moniker, John Cabot, and who sailed far enough into the North Atlantic in 1497 to reach a lonely beach in the Maritimes. Cabot stayed ashore only long enough to claim that beach's pebbles (he may have been in Newfoundland or he may have been in Cape Breton) for his patron. But back in England he dined out for months on tipsy promises to fellow publicans that when he returned to the New World he would name an island for them. He sailed west again with aims of tacking a bit farther to the south, but never came home. Which is how it fell to another mariner from the Italian peninsula, this one sponsored by the regent of France, to be recalled as the first European to enter New York Harbor—or to return, anyway, to tell the tale.

Given that claim to fame, you might think that Giovanni de Verrazzano has been continually famous ever since. But that bold Florentine, who visited the Harbor in 1524, didn't stay long before continuing down the coast. Most New Yorkers wouldn't know his name if it weren't for the patrons and members of the Italian Historical Society of America, who fought to see it stuck on a mighty suspension bridge that opened in 1964, to join Brooklyn to Staten Island, and which would soon play a starring role in *Saturday Night Fever*. Their cause was aided by the fact that several thousand Italian Americans in Bay Ridge, Brooklyn, were displaced by the bridge's building. They prevailed over rival proposals, including a perhaps less-convincing one from their Norwegian neighbors, also numerous in South Brooklyn, to see the span named for Leif Erikson instead. The city's inexplicable misspelling of their hero's name on the Verrazano-Narrows Bridge (its missing "z" was finally added in 2018) was perhaps a small price to pay for seeing at least one name from southern Europe enter the modern nomenclature and older origin story of a nation long eager to trace its varied roots to their Anglo aspects alone.

Henry Hudson, the first Englishman to angle a ship through Verrazzano's Narrows, did so while working for the Dutch. Which is why, after Hudson sailed up a broad river that the Mahicans called Muheconnetuk ("river that flows both ways") in 1609, he named that river Mauritius. This was an attempt to honor Maurice of Nassau, a prominent Dutch noble, but it seems to have gone unappreciated by the soldier-sailors of the Dutch West India Company who turned up a few years later to exploit Hudson's claim to what they called Noord Rivier (North River). This wasn't a very imaginative label, but it did make it easy for denizens of Nieuw Nederland (New Netherland) to distinguish it from their province's Zuyd Rivier (South River), which we know as the Delaware. By then, Henry Hudson, who was monomaniacal in his quest for the Northwest Passage, was no more: His frostbitten and mutinous crew, on an ice floe somewhere north of what's now Hudson Bay, chucked him to the walruses during an Arctic voyage in 1611. It wasn't until decades after they did so that the stout syllables of their captain's surname were attached, by New York's new English owners, to its principal river.

The town that the Dutch founded by that river's mouth, New Amsterdam, was from the start a very different place from the one launched around the same time by English Puritans by Massachusetts Bay. When a boatload of soldiers from Holland landed by Manhattan's southern tip to install an initial trading post there in 1613, but then sailed off for more supplies, they left in charge a mixed-race Latino from Hispaniola called Jan Rodrigues (or Juan Rodriguez, depending on your source) to man the fort till their return. From then on, New Amsterdam was a town devoted not to piety but to commerce, open to traders from everyplace. And Nieuw Nederland, the larger province of which it was a part, contrasted starkly with New England, whose main colonies were founded by pilgrims seeking their own religious freedom, but who countenanced no faith but Calvinism and whose followers would, soon enough, be executing people on charges of witchcraft.

Those contrasting visions and values competed and intertwined during the forty-plus years that the Dutch and English shared what's now the United States' Northeast—and then during the century between the English takeover of what they called New Netherland, in 1664, and an uprising against England's king that we call the American Revolution. Those tensions and ties colored the city's landscape as it gained first Dutch names and then English ones. And then, too, many odd mash-ups of the two that remain the most distinctive feature of a lived lexicon of place that I encounter whenever I leave my office at NYU. As I walk up the Bowery—an avenue whose name evokes street gangs and punk rock but which is now lined with boutiques selling $200 T-shirts, and whose name is an Anglicization of the Old Dutch term *bouwerij,* for a road leading to a farm—I approach a swish neighborhood whose name sounds appropriate to the London-style leafy square at its heart but doesn't come from London at all. "Gramercy," rather, derives from an English attempt to lend a more English-sounding gloss to what the Dutch called the area's "krom moerasje," or "crooked marsh." A man named Samuel Ruggles, who went on to become the city's commissioner of canals, drained this area in the 1830s to implant the stately town homes and elms of Gramercy Park.

FOR THE PLACE-NAME LOVER who wants a whiff of Old New Amsterdam in modern New York, the impulse might be to head first for Manhattan's southern tip. But the name-hound's nose, bringing them to where Dutch colonists built their town, would lead them wrong. The only place there that recalls the Dutch presence now is a little triangle of trees and concrete called Peter Minuit Plaza. It's a nice place to sip a Snapple while waiting to board the Staten Island Ferry, but it sits on landfill in what was, in Minuit's day, a nice place for a dip. To find the remnants of the old Dutch town nearby, one has to cross the street that once marked the water's edge, sensibly called Water Street, and enter a tangle of roads whose routes are Dutch and whose names' roots are, too, but which in the late 1600s became English. Once, those streets were Parelstraat (named for the bounty of oysters in the nearby East River) and Brugstraat, but now they're Pearl Street and Bridge Street. Nearby Wall Street has long been associated by a false etymology with the Dutch de Waal Straat (which actually meant "wharf street" and ran along the East River). The English occupiers took the obvious step of naming their Wall Street for its proximity to the palisade of sharpened timbers erected at New Amsterdam's northern edge in 1653 to defend the Dutch colony from the English. Other than these few examples, for direct reminders of the Dutch people whose lasting bequests to New York's culture include cookies, coleslaw, and stoops, you've got to venture beyond where their colonial enterprise began.

One reason for this is that their town's outlying areas remained rich, for decades and centuries after it became New York, with Dutch landowners and potentates—those varied Van Brunts and Van Cortlandts and Beekmans and Bleeckers whose names are now parks and roads and neighborhoods. Another reason is that other Dutch people also ventured, during New Amsterdam's brief forty-year life, beyond its walls to start farms and homesteads reachable by trotting up their *bouwerij,* or up another arterial byway that ran Manhattan's length and predated their presence.

That trail angled north from the Battery before coursing up Manhattan's West Side. It was called Wickquasgeck by the Lenape and dubbed Brede weg ("broad way") by the Dutch, before being carried into English as you-know-what. Broadway is still one way to reach a district of rock hills and low marshes that they named Nieuw Haarlem, after a prosperous town back home. In Holland, the area to old Haarlem's west was a florid district called Bloemendaal; they gave the same name to the bloom-filled valley to Nieuw Haarlem's west here. Thankfully, a later English attempt to rename the whole district "Lancaster" failed: We can be grateful to whatever wise souls chose to shorten Nieuw Haarlem to the pithier Harlem instead ("Lancaster Renaissance" just wouldn't have had the same ring) and to whatever forces, too, helped Bloemendaal become the Bloomingdale District, a now-antiquated label for the upper Upper West Side, which by happenstance shared a name with the German Jewish family behind the big department store that opened across town, in the late 1800s, on East 57th Street.

Two centuries before that happened, New Amsterdam's last and most important Dutch governor arrived to its piers from Curaçao, sporting a peg leg from his campaigns in the Caribbean and carrying orders, from his bosses in Amsterdam, to whip their North American colony into shape, and grow it, too. Between 1647 and when he handed his colony to the English seventeen years later, Peter Stuyvesant granted charters to five of his countrymen to found villages on the western end of Langue Eylandt (Long Island), now the borough of Brooklyn. To these, they gave names that either recalled old homes or described their new ones. The founder of Nieuw Utrecht was an investor from Utrecht, in Holland, whose hometown is now hailed, in southwest Brooklyn, by the name of New Utrecht Avenue and that of the alma mater— New Utrecht High School—of Bensonhurst notables including the mogul David Geffen and the mobster Joseph Colombo. (It was for one of New Utrecht's founding families, the Bensons, that Bensonhurst is named; another of those families was the Nostrands of Nostrand Avenue fame.) More descriptive Dutch village names were Boswijk (the "town in the woods" that's now Bushwick) and Midwout ("middle wood"). The latter settlement's name inspired that of modern Midwood, nearby, but was in fact located in what's now Flatbush (whose own name derives from an alternate Dutch tag for that zone: Vlacke Bos—"wooded plain"). Flatlands, by contrast, was born as the Dutch village of Nieuw Amersfoort before the English gave it a new name that was derived from no Dutch source at all but from their not-untrue observation that its environs were pretty flat.

The one village that the Dutch founded in what's now Queens was called Vlissingen, after a port town of that name back home. One understands, given a mouth feel that's more slippery than satisfying, why the English changed this one. But it became confoundingly evocative of toilets after they turned it into Flushing.

The most important of these villages, at least in terms of how its name has redounded since, was located across the water from New Amsterdam near what's now the bit of the DUMBO waterfront where tourists and lovers, framed by scenic bridges, take selfies. Breukelen was founded as a ferry landing for farmers in 1646. The English version of that name lent its syllables to what became the city's most populous borough, and after four centuries of urbanization "Brooklyn" is now also the name of a notorious street gang in Port-au-Prince, Haiti, and of insipid restaurants and boutiques, trading on long-distance imaginings of hipster cachet, from Auckland to Paris. But long before any of that, Breukelen was and remains a town of Gouda-munchers outside Amsterdam, known for nothing much.

SUCH PROCESSES AS THESE—the ways a place-name from one culture can be retained or transformed in another, before taking on a range of new associations and meanings in a third (or more)—are of keen interest to toponymists, and should be of more interest to all historians of culture. One other such set of place-names are false cognates—terms comprising the same sequence of letters in different languages, which, when spoken or written in one or the other, can bear wholly different meanings. It's hard to say whether English familiarity with their word "kill" is the sole factor that encouraged them, when they took over New Netherland and found Dutch maps full of that term, to mostly leave it be. It is also true that when one culture takes over a landscape previously occupied by another one, names for natural features seem to be left alone more often than names for human-made ones are. But leaving "kill" in place and even adopting it for themselves is what the English indeed did, to the amused concern of generations of kids. I can't be the only one who asked my parents, when we drove to visit my granddad in New Jersey via the Staten Island Expressway: Why *is* New York's biggest garbage dump called Fresh Kills?

The answer, as any schoolkid in Staten Island could have told me, is that "kill" is just an Old Dutch term for "creek" that's still stuck to the Arthur Kill that separates their borough from Jersey; to the Bronx Kill, which does the same between its borough and Randall's Island; and that vital curved watercourse, the Kill Van Kull, upon which all freighters heading to Newark Bay must float beneath the Bayonne Bridge. Up in Dutchess County, the name of Fishkill may conjure images of a stinky genocide of trout, but its name describes not a place for killing fish but a brook full of live ones. The Catskills' name combines that of a Lenape sachem in the area, called Cats, and a recognition that its slopes babbled with many streams. Down near what's now Philadelphia, in what were once New Netherlands' southern parts, the Dutch impact was large enough for them to leave behind their name for the Schuylkill ("hidden river")—but maybe not large enough for that name's inheritors to absorb what "kill" meant: They still refer to its waters by the redundant "Schuylkill River" ("hidden river river"). Not so in New York, where English farmers seem to have embraced the term with enough precision to affix it not merely to Dutch Kills in Queens, in the 1800s, but to two creek-crossed areas of southern Staten Island—Great Kills and Fresh Kills— whose names sound like murderous trophy grounds, perhaps aptly in the case of the biggest landfill on earth, for the most murderous society this planet's ever seen.

Another Dutch landscape term that reminded the English of a word of their own was "hoek." It means a promontory or spit of land, but was also a term that wasn't hard to translate, both phonetically and imagistically, into "hook." Along what's now Brooklyn's eastern shore, the Dutch attached a chromatic pair of modifiers to two such places—Roode Hoek (Red Hook, named for the red hue of that peninsula's clay) and Geel Hoeke (Yellow Hook, for the sulfuric hew of its)—whose names the English kept. Red Hook is still the name for a seaside neighborhood long known for its public housing projects and its artists, but more lately for IKEA. Yellow Hook stayed in use for a couple of centuries before a yellow fever epidemic in the area, in 1843, gave it an insensitive ring and the name was binned. Now it's Bay Ridge.

It makes sense that such cognates or near cognates should serve as inducements, for a successor culture, to keep its predecessors' place-words. But other names retain their best chance of staying put by pulling off what one might think of as their equivalent of shooting the moon—a feat achieved by names that are so unique-sounding, or uncannily apt to the spots they describe, that they grow impossible to change. Who, for example, could now dream of touching Spuyten Duyvil? That lovely Dutch-sounding name describes where, by the Bronx's southwest tip, the Harlem River's eddies touch the Hudson. It's grown familiar to generations of commuters who, rumbling up the Henry Hudson Parkway or on trains leaving Manhattan from Grand Central now associate its charming syllables—spoken, they sound like "Spy-ten Die-ville"—with antique-looking apartments and lovely river views. So attached are they to the name's sounds, one suspects, that their contents might surprise. For Spuyten Duyvil's singing consonants mask a meaning that's in fact quite menacing: the devil's whirlpool.

THERE ARE TWO WAYS, traditionally, that a human who aspires to have their name one day label a public place or thoroughfare might see that happen. One is by achieving great things that a whole lot of people, or at least the right people with the right kinds of power, deem great enough to wish to recall forever. The second is to own lots of land. It's by the latter means that the only one of New York's boroughs to be named for a person got that way. The name of the Bronx dates from the Dutch era but doesn't derive, aptly enough for a Dutch colony whose populace was never more than half Dutch, from a Dutchman: Jonas Bronck, who bought the boondocks north of Manhattan and built a homestead there in 1639, was a Dane. Mr. Bronck didn't do much to shape the history of the borough that would become the birthplace of hip-hop and J-Lo and the Yankees and AOC. But karma smiled rather more kindly on him, on account of his real estate, than on the rather more accomplished Dutchman for whom the riverside city of Yonkers, just over the county line in Westchester, is indirectly named.

That citizen, Adriaen van der Donck, was a jurist and writer who was sent to the New World by a prominent jewel merchant in Amsterdam, Kiliaen van Rensselaer, who was also a cofounder of the Dutch West India Company. In 1631, van Rensselaer purchased a vast tract of land by the Noord Rivier near what the Dutch called Fort Oranje and we call Albany. He hired Van der Donck, freshly graduated from Leiden University, to go to America and work as the lawman of a personal fief he never visited but which was called Rensselaerwyck. Once Van der Donck arrived, though, he spent less time tending his boss's holdings than reveling in the American landscape and communing with the native people, as he recorded in his landmark *A Description of New Netherland.* Then he moved south to New Amsterdam and became a signal figure in its early political and cultural history. Van der Donck was the best-educated man in the major North American colony of what was, in the seventeenth century, Europe's most cultured nation—nearly half the world's books, in those days, were printed in Holland. And he became that colony's leading voice for involving its populace in making decisions usually left, in the colonies of the Dutch West India Company, to directors appointed by the company. Russell Shorto, in his bestselling history of New York's Dutch era, *The Island at the Center of the World,* drew on newly translated documents from its colonial archives to describe Van der Donck as "the man who, more than any other . . . mortared together the foundation stones of a great city."

One might think, given these distinctions, that Van der Donck's name might feature as prominently on New York's modern map as that of the corporate manager, Peter Stuyvesant, who became his bête noire (and whose name now labels not merely an angled street that once led to his farm off the Bowery, but big housing projects and parks, a prestigious high school, and a fast-gentrifying area of Brooklyn called Bed-Stuy, short for Bedford-Stuyvesant). But not so for Van der Donck. His estate's sawmill inspired the name of the river by which it sat, Saw Mill

Creek, and also, much later on, of the Saw Mill Parkway. But his name is nowhere—unless you count the town whose name derives from the fact that, as a young Dutch gentleman of property, he achieved the title of Jonker or Jonkheer, the lowest rank of Dutch nobility. Which is why and how his land became known as Jonker's, and was called that even after he died, until the English gave it a name—Yonkers—that sounds like it must be related to that of the Bronx's favorite baseball team. Which, in a tenuous way, it might be: Some historians think "yankee" derived from Janke, a diminutive of the common Dutch first name Jan, which in Anglicized form became a nickname, at first derogatory but later less so, for both Dutch and English "colonials" across the northeast.

To picture how those wood-shoe-wearing Jonkers and Jankes lived, in New York's once-rural hinterlands, there's a constellation of landmarked homes one can visit that were built from timber and stone in the seventeenth and eighteenth centuries and once sat in fields but are now ringed by asphalt. Among them is the swoop-roofed Dyckman Farmhouse in upper Manhattan; Van Cortlandt House in the Bronx; and, straddling the frontier between Ridgewood, Queens, and Bushwick, Brooklyn, the Onderdonk House, whose whitewashed-stone exterior was long used to calibrate the two boroughs' border. Out in Flushing, Bowne House is a nexus for history clad in mustard shingles that's served variously, down the centuries, as a meeting place for the Quakers who in 1657 penned the "Flushing Remonstrance" to uphold toleration of all faiths in New Netherland; as home to the Bowne family, who became, after intermarrying with the Parsons clan in the early 1800s, the first family of American horticulture; and as a vital station, thanks to their abolitionist views, on the Underground Railroad. Few corners of the city boast so much history as that bit of Queens where the old Friends Meeting House (c. 1694) is down the block and so, too, is the landmarked home of Lewis Latimer, the African-American inventor who made the filament, a couple centuries later, that let Thomas Edison's lightbulb glow. But my favorite of the city's old homes to visit is the oldest of them all—and the most charmingly un-preserved.

Called Lent-Riker-Smith Homestead, it dates from 1654. It's named for the same family as the island off Queens, Rikers Island, that began serving as Gotham's city jail in the 1930s, and it occupies an acre-sized lot not far from LaGuardia Airport, in East Elmhurst, next to a Thrifty dealership and right near the causeway over which paddy wagons stamped with the slogan of the correctional officers' union ("New York's Boldest") carry the luckless. The house is a handsome wood-framed number with an old oak door painted red, in the Dutch style, for luck. Set amid sycamores and surrounded by low-rise blocks of homely mid-twentieth-century housing that evoke Archie Bunker, the home was first built by Abraham Rycken von Lent, a Dutch settler of means who would go on, a few years later, to buy the nearby island that bears his name's Anglicized form. But despite the noteworthy age of old Abraham's manse, it's not a place administered by the Parks Service or a devoted nonprofit. Instead, it's lived in, as it has been continually since the seventeenth century, by an heir or relation of the Riker clan—a role filled, nowadays, by a woman named Marion Duckworth Smith. Ms. Duckworth Smith maintains a website, at www.rikerhome.com, on which she invites persons interested in touring her house to drop her a line.

On the summer day after I did so, I arrived in East Elmhurst to find Ms. Duckworth Smith standing, in what looked like a gold lamé blazer, under an ancient gate whose letters spelled out RIKER in wrought iron. She led me, behind her home, through a family graveyard whose lichen-and-ivy-covered headstones included one for a Riker who'd died at Valley Forge and one for a retired veterinarian who lived on the grounds, she said with practiced precision, with forty-seven dogs and thirty-two cats. Then she showed me into a house whose wide-plank floors and pine staircase felt colonial indeed, but whose every surface and cranny she'd packed not with items from the 1600s or 1700s, but with all manner of totems of the more recent past—a wooden horse from the first carousel at Coney Island, family photos from World War I, an 1888 Steinway Grand ("made right here in Queens!"). As a keen lover of Broadway, she had also included, in the personal museum she felt compelled to create by her historic home, memorabilia from the Great White Way, including Carol Channing's necklace from *Hello, Dolly!* and Chita Rivera's sequined cabaret shoes. "I wore them once to a Broadway Cares fundraiser," she said, smiling with pride. "Chita saw them and said, 'Love your shoes.'"

TODAY THE WORD "COLONIAL" is more often used to describe furniture, in common parlance, than to name practices tied to seizing land or exploiting natives. Unless you're on a college campus where students use "colonial" as a synonym for evil, you're more likely to see the word attached to a chair or subdivision or house meant to register as assuredly old-fashioned—or as reminiscent of settlers from one or other of the European nations that did the colonizing in these parts. It's not a word, at least in the United States, that much distinguishes between varied colonial powers, and the different ideas and traditions— and names—that they left behind. But in the colonial history of New York, few moments are so key as the August day in 1664 when Richard Nicolls arrived at the head of four British ships, furnished by the Duke of York, to blockade New Amsterdam and inform its governor that the town was now his. Peter Stuyvesant, ten days later, peacefully surrendered. It was a development, in global terms, that signaled the rise of the British Empire and the decline of the Dutch one. In local terms, it marked the official start of a new chapter in New York's history—the era of the English—which had also, in key ways, already begun.

The town Nicolls took over was, like its namesake city in Holland in the seventeenth century, a place where refugees and strivers from across Europe—Walloons and Jews, Huguenots and Sicilians, Viennese and Danes— came to find fortunes and freedom. Many of those people, back in Amsterdam, had boarded Dutch West India Company boats using "Batavianized" last names to disguise their birth: The populace of the colony—which also contained several hundred enslaved Africans (many of whom took the surname Angola)—looked a lot like that of the city it would become. And New Netherland was also home, beginning in the 1630s, to not a few Englishmen and -women who'd left home to live or worship as they wished, only to fall out with New England's strict Puritan leaders and leave.

Prominent among these refugees was Anne Hutchinson, a brave midwife-cum-radical-theologian who grew notorious for insisting to a growing number of disciples in Massachusetts that the Holy Ghost wasn't only summoned earthward when they performed good works, but dwelled in them always. Her Antinomian teachings may have anticipated Pentecostalism and other born-here religions that eventually made catching the spirit as American as country music and civil rights, but John Winthrop's ministers weren't having it. Jailed and then convicted of sedition and devilry, Hutchinson left the colony with her husband and seven children. She headed first for Providence Plantations, the refuge of fellow Massachusetts outcast Roger Williams that became Rhode Island, and then for New Netherland, whose corporate directors cared much less about devilry than about economic development—and who in the era of Kieft's War with the Indians, especially, were extra-amenable to seeing the countryside settled by willing whites. Hutchinson obliged by acquiring land for her family in what's now the northeast Bronx, from a fellow English exile from New England: John Throckmorton, from whom we get our name for Throgs Neck. She didn't get to live there long before a band of Siwanoys killed her family. But it was long enough for the nearby Hutchinson River to be named for her and to then lend its tag, a couple of centuries on, to a parkway best known to commuters as the Hutch.

The name of Lady Deborah Moody isn't attached to any parkways and so passes modern New Yorkers' lips less often. But in 1643, Moody—an Anabaptist who fell into her own hot water in New England and chose excommunication over renouncing her faith—sought and was granted permission, by New Amsterdam's governor, to colonize Long Island's southwest tip. Thus were old Brooklyn's five Dutch villages joined by an English one whose original street layout one can glimpse around Lady Moody Square, in the modern neighborhood that has her village's name. You might think its moniker, Gravesend, has something to do with cemeteries, but in fact it derives from Lady Moody's evident fondness for the Thames-side English town of the same name, in Kent (whose name's origins some English toponymists suggest is an old bastardization of a medieval label meaning "end of the grove," while others suggest it derives from *graaf-ham*—the home of the reeve, or bailiff, of the Lord of the Manor).

The debate over that Old English place-name is hardly uncommon in a country where many such words reach back to the dark ages or earlier. But not a few English place-names grow intelligible if you familiarize yourself with the generic descriptive terms, pulled from Anglo-Saxon or Old Norse or otherwise, that are their basis—after one absorbs, that is, that every *-ton* is a town, every *-bury* is a fortified enclosure, and every *-ham* is, or was, a homestead. Throw in the truth that every *-stead* is a fenced field of some sort (including the town of Hempstead, on Long Island, which began life as a Dutch village whose name—Heemstede—doubtless reminded Englishmen of a pretty park in north London) and you're on the way to being able to parse a good many English town names on either side of the pond.

After taking New Amsterdam, Richard Nicolls chose to keep its name's first word ("New"), but to swap in, for its second, that of his patron. Then he and his successors imported many boring names from Britain—Suffolk, Kensington, Westchester—and named not a few other key places and bits of infrastructure, especially once the Duke of York became King James II, for their monarchs. These included the counties of Queens and Kings (aka Brooklyn), and a new name for what was once the Dutch town of Wiltwijck, up the Hudson: Kingston. Nowadays, Kingsbridge is a neighborhood in the Bronx. Once it was a wooden trestle that brought horsemen and travelers from Manhattan toward points north and the old Boston Road, which hung a right near Pelham (that is, the old homestead of the Pells) and arced into New England and toward Boston along a route that tracks pretty closely with today's I-95. The English were also often content to simply tweak Dutch names until they sounded English, turning Conyne Eylandt ("rabbit island") into Coney Island, and Staaten Eylandt (which means "states' island," in honor of Holland's States-General) into Staten Island. In 1671 there, Dutch residents of a settlement they called their "dorp," or village, decided to build a new such settlement nearby. The English gave to their old town the official name Old Dorp and gave their new one a tag it still has: New Dorp.

No one would ever accuse the English, in their place-naming habits, of being great lovers of nature. But they did allow themselves to be inspired by local fauna to forge place-names like the ones they gave a pair of watery inlets, one on Manhattan's east side and the other off southern Brooklyn, that they named for turtles and sheepsheads, respectively. The name of the latter place, Sheepshead Bay, may call to mind a butcher's grisly leavings. Nowadays it's a waterside enclave of Brooklyn Russians where in winter I love to take the Q train to a banya whose hot baths are ringed, on the wall, with hockey jerseys. But its bay's name was actually inspired by a now-extinct but decidedly frightening-looking fish with human-like teeth (give them a Google) that once swam there in abundance.

England in the seventeenth and eighteenth centuries was becoming a global empire whose owners and officers also liked naming new places for other colonies or ports of call they'd passed through or from whose natives or slaves they'd made stacks of cash. They succeeded in giving such a name to Jamaica, Queens. In an area of what's now Hackensack that one Englishman tried to name New Barbados, they didn't. Which is a pity for two reasons. The first is that it would be fantastic to have a part of Hackensack named New Barbados. The second is that the literal meaning of "Barbados" (Portuguese for "bearded ones") would have been appreciated by the large Portuguese community now residing in that part of New Jersey, who may or may not know that the reason the most English island in the Caribbean has a Portuguese name is that some sailors from Lisbon who alighted there en route to Brazil in the sixteenth century, before the English came to properly colonize it in the seventeenth, named it for the bearded fig trees amid which they camped for a few days in 1536.

DELANCEY AND MOORE, GRACIE and Beach, Rector and Trinity—New York's English period saw not a few streets named for its foremost families and churchmen. It also saw several streets gain names—Duke, George, King—that were common to English towns of that era the world over. The reason we don't now know or refer to these is that they were the first to be changed, after the American Revolution, by people who'd just fought a war to stop honoring a distant king. (Prince Street survived the purge.) But the Americans of those founding fathers' generation, like children who reject their parents but love Grandpa, seem to have been far more warmly disposed to names derived from the Old Dutch, to whom their kids, and ours, owe thanks for Santa Claus.

The American writer who turned the Dutch tradition of Saint Nicholas (called in Dutch Sint-Nicolaas, or Sinterklaas) into the chubby elf who now visits American malls was Washington Irving. Irving was more responsible than any citizen of the young United States for instilling in his countrymen an attachment to a Dutch past that was, in many ways, more imagined than real. Irving's self-declared aim, in his wildly popular tales about headless horsemen and Knickerbockers and denizens of Sleepy

Hollow, was to furnish Americans with a rough equivalent of "the tales which live like charms and spells about the cities of the Old World." And he succeeded. In 1809, Irving released his *History of New York from the Beginning of the World to the End of the Dutch Dynasty,* under the pen name Diedrich Knickerbocker. His pseudonym's surname—a colonial-era nickname for Dutch settlers, perhaps inspired by the way they liked rolling up their pants to just below the knee—became a symbol of New York with enough staying power to inspire the name of the city's pro basketball team in 1946. Few fans of that perpetually middling franchise, when they call WFAN to bewail its owners' latest shitty trade or overpaid star, are likely to imagine old Dutchmen in knickered pants when they do. But there's a reason that today's Knicks sport the same orange and blue colors, also worn by baseball's Mets, as the Netherlands' national soccer teams.

Irving's most popular story was published in 1819. "Rip Van Winkle" was set three years before the American Revolution in a village in the Catskills. It told the story of a Dutchman who wandered into the woods to gain some peace from his nagging wife and happened upon merry members of Henry Hudson's long-lost crew, in a mountain hollow playing nine-pins and drinking ale. Lying down there for a tipsy nap, he wakes twenty years later with a beard to his waist and shocked to find that his old neighbors are no longer pledging allegiance to King George III. "Rip Van Winkle" is a yarn about how transitions from one epoch to the next, although often rendered as tidily stark in timelines and history books, aren't ever experienced so discretely by people who live far from where treaties are signed. They've always known that epochs and cultures have a way, like zones of a water-color, of bleeding into each other. Rarely does a new era not emerge from seeds already present; never does a new era, thus born, not contain traces and structures and sounds from what's come before. Pockets of Dutch speak-ers persisted in the Hudson Valley until well into the nineteenth century—it was in one such that Sojourner Truth, the famous abolitionist and feminist, grew up speaking Dutch before she learned the tongue in which she proclaimed "Ain't I a Woman." She and others who were enslaved or killed in New York's colonial age can attest that many of its "charms and spells" were haunted by violence. But it was Washington Irving's achievement, at least, to turn the minds of his contemporaries toward what came before.

Americans have in general been much less good at sourcing their place-names from literature, George Stew-art claimed, than from history and myth and poppycock. But if exceptions prove rules, then it's telling that Irving isn't merely the only literary figure to have both a street in Manhattan (Irving Place) and a village in Westches-ter (Irvington) named after him. He's also the writer whose pen inspired the most wonderfully named piece of infrastructure in the Hudson Valley: the steel span that crosses the river between the towns of Catskill and Hudson, which, upon its opening to the public by Franklin Roosevelt's New York State Bridge Authority in 1935, was dubbed the Rip Van Winkle Bridge. There's no moment of the drive upstate that I love more than glimpsing signs for a bridge whose name can't but put one in mind of the drowsy old Dutchman who lay down for a nap and woke, under hickories and pines, to a new world.

4.

THE AMERICANS

If "colonial" is one word whose meaning is in the eye of the beholder, as a descriptor of eras and of home furnishings alike, "revolutionary" is another. When England's North American colonies became the first such outposts of Europe in the New World to turn themselves into a sovereign country, those words were both at issue.

The war by which that transformation occurred began as a revolt of men who'd tired of paying their taxes; it's recalled in this country as the American Revolution, but as it occurred, it was seen by people elsewhere—in England—as a colonial skirmish. The reason posterity tracks with the American version is that the party that was trying to upset the status quo emerged triumphant. That's how it's been with every "revolution" and "riot" and "civil war" in history: Winners, whether or not they write the history books, do get to name the violence they live. This we know. Less often pondered, with regard to

America's Revolution, is how a tussle which began with men refusing to pay their taxes became a righteous war, in their own minds at least, for aims no less noble than life and liberty and the right of humans to pursue happiness. But once that became the case, it also became a war that saw itself, as all revolutions do, as a radical break from the past. And such breaks from the past, especially when they birth a new nation on the world stage, need new names for the places where they happen.

Given that fact, and the general air of grandiosity and hubris attending this country's birth, it's long seemed curious that its founders couldn't come up with a less mundane name for it than the United States. Lovers of names and of the USA, ever since, have proposed alternatives. These have tended either to toast its ideals (Freedonia), or to hail, in a similar brand of Anglo-Latinish, Genoese explorers or founding fathers with now-declining reputations (Columbia, Jeffersonia). Given those options, we can perhaps be grateful that those founders went for mundanity. And beyond the moniker of the nation itself, in any case, the story of the Revolution left behind a lot of names.

The story of how and why it did so runs through New York in key ways. But it began on the town green of a village outside Boston, one spring morning in 1775. George Stewart narrated that dawn's drama, and its echoes' effects on American naming, with verve:

Then the firing came, and men lay dead upon the grass. The line wavered and broke, and perhaps some British officer thought: "Well, that's over!" Yet all day that news and that name spread outward from the village where women sat with their dead. Reuben Brown took the alarm west to Concord. It went east to meet the men of Salem and Marblehead, marching already . . . They fired . . . our men are dead . . . Lexington! A new name on the land! . . . In Connecticut men heard the name on Thursday, as the riders galloped . . . On Sunday morning, a rider clattered upon the cobbles of New York, and men marched in the streets shouting the new name . . . Still farther it went, the name of that little village. What riders carried it, no one knows . . . It took the Wilderness Road through Cumberland Gap. There at last in that western land, a thousand miles from that village green, it came in June to a camp of hunters. They heard the name and said, "Let us call this place Lexington."

Which is how the clearing where those hunters sat in the bluegrass, by what's now home to Kentucky's state university, got its name. It was the first of many Lexingtons, as Stewart writes. "For now there was a new name in the land, and children learned it with their first words.

At last the people had a symbol—not a stupid king across the ocean, but a name red with their own blood."

The sound and shade of names "red with their own blood"—this is what, in the end, revolutionaries want. A new reality, cast in their ideals' image, that trumpets who forged it—or who died, even better, in the doing. Martyrs and monuments have always been linked. And no earthly nation, especially among those that were once colonies and became free, hasn't named cities or rivers or key bits of infrastructure for key figures in its founding. The style of doing so has differed. Across Africa, in many ex-colonies that were reborn as countries after World War II, few bits of infrastructure have served as such potent symbols of modernity and development as airports: Countless countries have built or renamed theirs, during this period, for whichever Kenyatta or Nyerere or Tambo helped them come to be. Latin Americans, since the age of Bolívar, have been fond of hailing their countries' development with dates on the calendar. This is why if you ever find yourself, for example, in Havana and being directed by a friend or stranger to head from Diez de Octubre to 19 de Noviembre, you should know you're not being urged to hail a cab capable of time travel. You're being directed from a barrio in Cuba's capital to its main train station. (October 10 is the date in 1868, as every Cuban knows, when the island's fight for independence from Spain got under way; November 19 is the day, in 1837, when its first train did.) Here in gringo America, the custom of naming places for dates never took: If it had, lots of our towns would boast a July 4 Boulevard and another, hailing the date of what's celebrated as Patriots' Day in Massachusetts, called April 19 Avenue. What we have instead are spots, like Lexington Avenue on Manhattan's east side, named for where that war sparked. Twenty states, including Massachusetts and Kentucky, have a Lexington; twelve more have a Concord. Lots more are named for heroes, like the general who became the United States' first president and whose future as its heavyweight champion of place-names began in New York.

It was in April 1776 that George Washington, on a hill in northern Manhattan, supervised the building of a fort to prevent the British from sailing up the Hudson. That garrison, which was dubbed Fort Washington by the men guarding it, occupied land that's been known as Washington Heights since. That same summer, Washington was appointed commanding general of the Continental Army. And on July 9, 1776, on a patch of grass in lower Manhattan that was then called the Common and is now City Hall Park, he addressed that army's troops. Across the water in Staten Island, twenty thousand British soldiers were readying to attack. But Washington had the newly signed Declaration of Independence read aloud to his enthused charges. Ginned up on noble verbiage, they swarmed down to Bowling Green and pulled down a statue of George III. Though they may not have thought to chant "decolonize this place," that's what they wanted.

And Washington, facing the daunting task of defending Manhattan from the world's top navy, was encouraged by their ardor.

.

ARDOR, IN THE EVENT, wasn't enough to hold New York. Washington's defense of the city saw him direct his lieutenants to build forts, that summer, which included one on a grassy hill in what's now central Brooklyn whose commander and builder—General Nathanael Greene of Rhode Island—is recalled in the name of the modern neighborhood of Fort Greene. Fort Defiance, down in Red Hook by the water, didn't become a neighborhood. But its name does survive, at least, as that of a bar that's my favorite place in Brooklyn to order a burger with cheddar. Washington's defense also included a few deft moves. He famously stewarded thousands of men, after Long Island was lost, across the East River under cover of dark and fog, back to Manhattan. But by September, Admiral Richard Howe's redcoats had seized the colonies' most vital port. New York, which Washington considered burning to the ground before leaving it to Howe, was a hotbed of royalist sentiment with a populace generally much less patriotic than Boston's or Philadelphia's, and would remain British for the rest of the war.

Before Washington grew famous for his exploits, over ensuing years, at Valley Forge and Trenton and Yorktown, his family name suggested nothing more noble than a town for doing laundry in. In fact, it's a town in the north of England, near Newcastle, whose name perhaps derives from an old Anglo-Saxon word, "Hwæsingatūn," for "estate of the descendants of the wheat sheaf." A century and change after George's great-grandfather, John, brought that word to Virginia as his surname in 1656, "Washington" was made august-sounding indeed by the general who declined to become king. And now his name graces not merely our nation's capital and a big state in the Pacific Northwest, but also 32 counties, 8 mountains, 10 lakes, and no fewer than 121 cities and towns across America. There are three times as many Washingtons, in the United States, as Springfields (of which there are 41, not including the pretend one where Bart Simpson lives). And of course George's name is all over New York City, too, which his army retook in 1783. Washington Square Park, dedicated a few decades later, is joined in hailing his memory by Washington Streets in Manhattan, Brooklyn, and the Bronx, respectively. Washington Heights, where his fort's former location is marked by a street, Colonel Robert Magaw Place, named for the man he left to command it, is now less known for this history than for its baseball players, bachata on the radio, and a plethora of places, thanks to immigrants from the Dominican Republic who've settled here since the 1960s, that serve plates of mashed-plantain deliciousness they call mofongo. But since 1931 it's also been the neighborhood from whence the mighty George Washington Bridge, with its gray-green towers recalling his pate's color on one-dollar bills, has joined New York to North America.

On maps of that continent, Washington's name grew so pervasive and prominent after his death that he may be, thanks to the wealth and scale of the nation he midwifed, one of earth's most toponymically honored humans. And places named in Washington's honor aren't limited to here: Among the cities worldwide that boast a George Washington Avenue are Warsaw, Rome, and Santo Domingo. There in the Dominican capital, Avenida George Washington is a scenic oceanfront drive whose name survived even the thirty years during which the city was renamed Ciudad Trujillo, by a vile dictator whose regime motivated many of his countrymen and -women to migrate to New York. In their adopted hometown, old George is hardly the sole hero of his Revolution to be honored by street names in a city that, after the war, grew rapidly.

SUCH NAMES LIE ESPECIALLY thickly over the area of lower Manhattan that in the 1700s was the no-man's-land between its colonial port and Greenwich Village. Thompson and Sullivan, MacDougal and Mercer, Wooster and Broome—all are names, although the shoppers and tourists taking selfies on their sidewalks don't know it, that hail brave campaigners against the British. So does that of nearby Horatio Street, albeit by using its honored general's first name instead of his boring second one: Horatio Gates was an English officer turned American patriot who came out of retirement, in 1777, to win the Battle of Saratoga. Houston Street, the east–west drag that forms the northern edge of SoHo's grid of onetime sweatshops turned artists' lofts turned ridiculous boutiques, was named in 1808 for William Houstoun, Georgia's representative to the Continental Congress. (His namesake street lost its second "u" when a critical mass of city bureaucrats and directory writers, perhaps inspired by Sam Houston's exploits in Texas in the 1830s, changed its spelling to "Houston.") The place where Houston hits Varick has been known to city cinephiles, for a few decades now, as the locus of Film Forum. It's also a corner where one street named for a Georgian bisects one named for a New Yorker, Richard Varick, who served as General Washington's aide-de-camp. (Varick also later became New York's mayor.)

In the 1770s, Brooklyn was a still-rural district of windmills and farms with a population of no more than 3,500. It became notorious, during its wartime occupation by the British, for the rather larger number of American prisoners of war—some 12,000—who died as captives on one of the rat-infested brigs they kept anchored at Wallabout Bay by what's now the Brooklyn Navy Yard. (The Prison Ship Martyrs' Monument, in Fort Greene Park, hails their memory.) It's thanks to Washington's and Greene's early battles there, though, and to the truth that many of the borough's fields were turned into city streets while memories of the war were fresh (unlike in Queens and the Bronx, where this happened later), that Alfred Kazin, the borough's Depression-era bard of the BMT, could describe how "with each homey crash crash crash of the wheels against the wheels, there would steal up at me . . . all those streets in middle Brooklyn named after generals of the Revolutionary War."

Among those was Nathanael Greene, of course, and also Horatio Gates: In Brooklyn, his eponymous street isn't Horatio but Gates. Several other streets' names betrayed how the officer corps of the Continental Army, like modern Brooklyn's populace, was drawn from many lands. Johan de Kalb was a Bavaria-born soldier of French extraction who built his reputation battling the British in Europe before doing the same thing as a major general in Washington's army, and growing so admired by Americans that Tennessee and Texas and seven other states boast towns or counties called DeKalb—and Brooklyn's got DeKalb Avenue. Parallel to that thoroughfare, in Fort Greene, is one named for another French officer. The Marquis de Lafayette first crossed the Atlantic as De Kalb's young protégé but went on, over the war's course, to become an icon of *liberté* nearly as beloved in the young United States as Washington himself (and reciprocated American admiration by naming his own children George Washington and Virginie).

From even farther east in the Old World came

Tadeusz Kościuszko, the world-trotting Polish general and polymath who joined the Continental Army's cause in 1776, motivated by shared animus toward Britain, before masterminding several of its victories, designing forts like West Point, and becoming one of Thomas Jefferson's dearest pals. Then he returned home to become the foremost leader of the Polish-Lithuanian Commonwealth's campaign against Russian aggression, and wrote a will that left all his assets to the cause of freeing and educating America's slaves. Monuments to "the world's most popular Pole" include a man-made mountain in Krakow called Kościuszko Mound and a god-made one in New South Wales, Mount Kosciuszko, that is Australia's highest peak. They also include a recently rebuilt and refurbished bridge, between Brooklyn and Queens, that carries the Brooklyn-Queens Expressway over murky Newtown Creek. The spur for naming that vital span for Poland's foremost contributor to American liberty, in September 1940, came from recent events that menaced Poland's own. Mayor Fiorello La Guardia dedicated the bridge in front of thousands of Polish Americans, months after the Nazis took Warsaw. "Any land that breeds such lovers of freedom," the mayor proclaimed of Kościuszko, "can never be kept enslaved."

Another Polish lover of freedom was Casimir Pulaski, a dashing horseman and officer who won fame battling Prussians and Russians before he was invited in 1777 by Benjamin Franklin to fight the British in America and distinguished himself by saving George Washington's life at Brandywine and commanding his cavalry. Pulaski died in battle at Savannah, where Georgia's Pulaski County was named for him a century before his name was added to New York's streetscape. His namesake bridge opened in 1954, just down Newtown Creek from Kościuszko's, to connect Long Island City to Greenpoint, Brooklyn, a neighborhood whose recent gentrification hasn't totally obscured the signs—in Polish churches and emporia of pierogis and slivovitz that can't be beat—of its historic stature as the city's great mecca of Polishness.

Nearby Williamsburg, which in the twenty-first century has become a mecca of nothing so much as recent NYU grads having their parents cosign leases on pricey flats, was the brainchild, in the early nineteenth, of a ferry operator named Woodhull. He bought thirteen acres of farmland in 1802 that he hired engineer Jonathan Williams to cut up into streets. It was thanks to Mr. Williams, a West Point man who was also a great-nephew of Benjamin Franklin, that many of his burg's byways were named for signers of the Declaration of Independence. Clymer, Ellery, Gerry, Hart; Harrison, Hooper, Heyward, Hewes; Ross, Rush, Rutledge, Penn—they're all names belonging to one or another of those fifty-six men who scrawled their letters at the Declaration's base. So are Taylor and Thornton, Wythe and Whipple.

William Whipple of New Hampshire, a brigadier general during the war, was also a merchant and sea captain who shipped enslaved Africans to Portsmouth and owned them, too: his namesake street is one of seventy, across Brooklyn, that honor slave owners. (His slave Prince Whipple fought by Washington's side and is the only person of color depicted in that famous painting of Washington crossing the Delaware.) John Williams's uncle Ben, who at the age of seventy was the Declaration's oldest signer in 1776, naturally has a street in Brooklyn: Franklin Street there is joined in recalling that outstanding citizen of the proto-republic by Franklin Streets in Manhattan, the Bronx, and Staten Island. Keap Street is a thoroughfare, like many in South Williamsburg today, where hipster-patronized tattoo parlors and taquerias jostle for space with the Orthodox yeshivas of old-guard Hasidim. Its name does not match that of one of the Declaration's signers, but it tries to: "Keap" is apparently a misrendering of the surname of the last man to leave his mark on it: Thomas McKean of Pennsylvania, whose name's illegibility was perhaps due to his having rather less space to scrawl it by the time the document reached him than John Hancock did.

Back in Manhattan, the name "Madison Avenue" may put one in mind of the ad execs of *Mad Men,* but of course it was named for the same Virginia-born drafter of the Constitution whose name also graces Madison Square and, by extension, the home arena of the Knicks. James Madison and James Monroe were as congruent in their initials as in the home state they also shared with Thomas

Jefferson, and are just as proximate on city maps as on timelines of U.S. presidents (whereon Jefferson, as you may recall from seventh-grade history, was third, Madison fourth, and Monroe fifth) as on maps of New York. In Brooklyn, Monroe Street, Madison Street, and Jefferson Street are bunched together closely; the same is true of three identically named streets on Manhattan's Lower East Side. And not far from where they are, you'll find an avenue running parallel to the Bowery that was named, in 1825, for the Marquis de Lafayette. By then, the famous Frenchman had already seen his name attached to many places, beginning with Fayetteville, North Carolina, in 1783. But in 1825 he returned to America, as an old man, for a grand tour that saw America gain many more places called Lafayette—there are now some seventy-two of those in the United States, including towns and townships and cities—and his surname added to squares and schools and avenues in many more. Among them was Lafayette Street in Manhattan, which is perhaps now best known as the home of the Public Theater. Since 1967, "the Public" has been based in the red-brick Romanesque pile that once housed the Astor Library. In 2015 it hosted the opening of a musical production toasting the life of the most prominent New Yorker among America's founding generation, which went on to become the country's most popular musical in decades.

.   .   .

IT MAKES ALL KINDS of sense that that New Yorker, Alexander Hamilton, was both an immigrant from the Caribbean and a fast-talking financier with street smarts who died in a duel. Long before Lin-Manuel Miranda turned his biography into inspired fodder for a hip-hop-laced opera about America's birth, Hamilton's name was hallowed here: It's attached to Hamilton Heights and Hamilton Grange in Harlem; to Fort Hamilton in Brooklyn; to a town and a liberal arts college upstate known for its hockey team. Hamilton's roles in helping Washington run the Continental Army and as a young lawyer who helped ratify the Constitution are well known. But his larger legacies, in what became America's capital of finance, grew from his creating the United States' first bank, in New York, and then by going on, as Washington's first secretary of the Treasury, to found the First Bank of the United States. Building a new nation, Hamilton believed, required financial organs able to extend large loans, funded by selling shares in their assets-to-be called "scrips," to both its citizens and their government.

To rural republicans like Thomas Jefferson, whose own wealth derived less from bits of paper than from his estate's acreage and his slaves' toil, such monetary make-believe smelled fishy. He warned that allowing New York's financiers to control the nation's wealth would amount to "an infinity of felonious larcenies." That's a quote that critics of Wall Street love reciting at moments when its greed begets ruinous crises. But Jefferson lost his argument with Hamilton. Banking was enshrined with the Bill of Rights as central to the secular creed of a country whose citizens, remarked the flamboyant New York banker Jacob Barker, were typified by an "inordinate appetite for gain." And city financiers like Barker, who in the early 1800s helped invent what came to be called "investment banking," would prove vital, in literally concrete ways, to New York's explosive growth.

Nothing abetted that growth more than the mighty infrastructure project, funded by the state with the help of bonds issued by city banks, that linked America's great port to its heartland's vast resources. The Erie Canal was opened in 1825 by Governor DeWitt Clinton, who poured a cask of water from Lake Erie into the waves off Sandy Hook to signal "the joining of the waters." Clinton's name is now not merely a neighborhood in Brooklyn (Clinton Hill), but a pair of Avenues (Clinton and DeWitt), too. On the west side of Manhattan, DeWitt Clinton Park is ringed by a neighborhood once known as Clinton and also boasts, alongside its benches and oaks, DeWitt's Dog Run. DeWitt Clinton High School, in the Bronx, counts among its distinguished alumni a Jewish photographer from that borough and a black writer from Harlem: Years before Richard Avedon and James Baldwin forged their famous careers, they met as teens working on the school paper at Clinton. Across the city in Red Hook, Brooklyn, the Bush-Clinton Playground wasn't named to commemorate the presidential election of 1992. Its moniker derives from its location at the intersection of two streets whose names long predate George H. W. Bush, Bill Clinton, and their families' rise to political prominence. One of those streets was named for a bygone landowner named Bush, the other for old DeWitt Clinton.

A similar backstory to the governor's great canal, and lots more bond financing, shaped the development of Manhattan's signature grid. With its numbered lattice of streets and avenues modeled on Philadelphia's similar system, but laid out along vastly more ambitious lines in 1811, the grid necessitated dynamiting hills and draining many marshes. The Commissioners' Plan that outlined the rationale for doing so was partly written by Gouverneur Morris, who wasn't a governor, but was the scion of a wealthy family whose old estate's acreage, in the Bronx, is recalled by the neighborhood name Morrisania. Morris had also penned the preamble to the U.S. Constitution, and now he made another appeal, in propounding the virtues of rectilinear urban planning, to truths he thought self-evident. "A city is to be composed principally of the habitations of men," he wrote, "and . . . straight-sided and right-angled houses are the most cheap to build and the most convenient to live in."

MORRIS HAD A POINT. And in the great city built along the lines he propounded there was much attention paid, in those first decades after the Revolution, to expunging traces of Englishness, or loyalty to English royals at any rate, from its physical plant. This was done in many ways. The first was the simplest. It involved erasing from the streetscape traces of the ancien régime. Not a few of New York's august colonial families, thanks to the Confiscation Act passed during the war, were relieved of their property: among them were the De Lanceys, who lost their big farm on Manhattan's east side but did see a road marking its location, called Delancey, survive. So did the namesake lane, nearby, of the publisher of the city's leading loyalist newspaper: Rivington Street survived the purge on account of the blockbuster news, after the war, that James Rivington had also served as a secret agent for the Continental Army. But among the old addresses wiped from lower Manhattan's map in 1794 were Crown Street (it became Liberty Street), King George Street (which became a part of William Street), and both Little Queen Street and Great Queen Street—which were, in fact, not two streets at all, but rather a sequential pair of blocks on the road now called Cedar.

This last renaming, which was also a consolidation, expressed another abiding aim of these Americans: to transcend, in matters of place-naming and otherwise, the Old World's inefficient ways. Their desire for new customs, user-friendly and redolent of progress, saw them do away with the old English habit of having urban streets change their name every block. This practice, which is still confounding visitors to London today, wouldn't do in their new land of reason. They resolved, as an expedient to correspondence and to commerce, to effect a change that also altered their descriptions of locations in the city. Where in Britain you might still be told, when asking a friend where they live, that they reside "*in* King Street," New Yorkers began conceiving of their streets, whether they ran a few blocks or a few miles, as more like rivers than places. Which is why Americans still describe their home streets using the same preposition that they would if they were so fortunate as to live in a house that overlooks, or is "on," the Hudson or the Rhine. New Yorkers don't say that they live in Broadway or in Bleecker Street. They say that they live on them.

This system, in alliance with the numbered grid that later spread beyond Manhattan to the Bronx (the town of Morrisania, which in 1855 gave its east–west streets numbers corresponding with Manhattan's, was the first to anticipate its eventual incorporation into greater New York), has certainly been a boon to navigation. It's why New York taxi drivers, even before the advent of talking GPS units on their dashboards, have never been obliged, as their black-cab brethren in London still are, to pass a test as a prerequisite of their profession. London cabbies, by contrast, must learn by heart "The Knowledge," which includes the ability to locate each of the thirty-one streets in London called Queens Road, the thirty-four named Victoria Road, and the dozens of names by which such byways are also known as they course around and through Britain's higgledy-piggledy capital, past blocks called Burnieboozle Crescent and Pie Corner and Whirligig Lane.

Of course, rationalism can go too far. As convenient as Manhattan's grid may be for getting around, the jury may still be out—especially to jurors hailing from across the sea—about its capacity for helping one know, in a deeper sense, where one is. A century and more after Lafayette attended his namesake street's unveiling, another world-famous Frenchman appraised the numbered streets and avenues. Jean-Paul Sartre's remark, on visiting Manhattan, was that "I am never astray, but always lost." Over the years, decades of activity and habit and incident—to say nothing of songs, from the Ramones' "53rd and 3rd" to Bob Dylan's "Positively 4th Street" to Bobby Womack's "Across 110th Street"—have lent some of those coordinates meanings more lyrical than logistical.

But the American psyche forged when King George was forced to relinquish his colonies has long combined the desire to leave old countries behind with a desire, at least as strong, to recall the Old World's charms. America's Revolutionary generation may have been determined to rid New York's streets of their old English owners, but America's ownership classes never abandoned their Anglophiles' love, as H. L. Mencken noted in *The American Language,* for attaching Old English–sounding synonyms for street—"court," "close," "drive," "place"—to their new American blocks.

This habit of street-naming was much in evidence in the Tudor-revival subdivisions and other early suburbs that developers in the late nineteenth and early twentieth centuries implanted in the erstwhile fields of what are now the outer boroughs. After the old towns of Queens agglomerated into one sprawling entity in 1898, they also received a gridded master plan. It wasn't nearly as easy to complete or execute as Manhattan's was. Surveyor Charles Powell, confronting many old numbered roads and redundancies among the borough's communities, sought to meld them all, in 1911, into a coherent whole. One means he devised for doing so was to give every street address in Queens a two-part number to signal its coordinates: 64-43 108th in Forest Hills (which happens to be the address of the neighborhood's go-to spot for kosher Chinese, Cho-Sen Garden) is on 108th Street at 64th Road. More confusingly, he allowed numbers to be repeated, by like-numbered roads with different names. This is why Kew Gardens, for example, boasts not merely a 72nd Avenue but a 72nd Road, 72nd Drive, and 72nd Crescent. It's also why poor Maspeth, where the grids of several surrounding communities come together, is such a confounding spaghetti bowl of numbers where you could, if you fancied, tell a friend to meet you at the intersection of 65th Place, 62nd Street, and 52nd Avenue—which you've got to be sure not to mistake for 52nd Court, nearby.

The use of regal-sounding synonyms for "street" is also glimpsed in the archipelago of spots across the city named by or for the family that became its wealthiest. John Jacob Astor, that family's patriarch, was born Johann Jakob Astor in Walldorf, Germany, in 1763, and immigrated to New York as a young man. He got rich shipping boatloads of beaver felt, coveted for making top hats, back to Europe and around the world, and then he grew his family's fortune with the epic swaths of city real estate that earned him and his progeny renown as "the landlords of New York." Among the Astors' namesake streets, in a city whose post-Revolutionary royalty were defined not by bloodline but by cash, were Astor Court, Astor Row, and Astor Place. Astor Avenue, in the Bronx, was where the family stabled their horses. Their palace for the paying public, in Midtown Manhattan, was the Waldorf-Astoria Hotel. And although that luxe hostelry, which gave the world the Waldorf salad and Thousand Island dressing, may no longer be American owned (in 2014, it was bought by Chinese insurance giant Anbang), that's not the case with the neighborhood of Astoria, Queens. It got its name in 1840, when the founders of a newly incorporated village by Queens' northwest edge decided to name it in honor of John Jacob Astor.

Their hope was that doing so might convince the rich old man, whose Manhattan mansion they could see across the East River, to give them money. All they ever got out of Mr. Astor, who never set foot in his namesake town, was $500. But over the ensuing century of industrialization and growth, Astoria became known for the

Steinway piano factory that opened there in 1872 on a huge four-hundred-acre campus with its own schools, churches, and amusement park; for the motion picture studios that opened near its southern end in the early 1900s, before that industry moved to Hollywood; and for Irish and Jewish and Italian immigrants who landed here straight from Ellis Island, to work in those studios or as butchers or tailors or grocers. Astoria became known, later on, for the jazz-loving son of one of those grocers, a Calabrian immigrant named Benedetto, who changed his name to Tony Bennett and became a famous singer. And it also became known—after migration laws changed in 1965 and southern Europe's ancient cradle of democracy descended into civil war—for tens of thousands of Greeks from Athens and Cyprus and the Peloponnese, who by the 1970s made meaty stretches of Ditmars Boulevard and 23rd Avenue the city's go-to blocks for Retsina wine and Kalamata olives, and for Amygdalou almond sponge cake at the Omonia Café. (The Omonia, along with much of Greek Astoria, later moved down to Broadway.)

YOU MAY READ ON the Internet that Ditmars was named for either Abram Ditmars, who in 1870 became the first mayor of the short-lived municipality of Long Island City (of which Astoria was then a part), or for Raymond Lee Ditmars, a renowned herpetologist who served for many years as head of reptiles at the Bronx Zoo. In fact, the boulevard was named, in 1915, with a nod to the mayor, but mainly for those modern Ditmarses' forebears: the old German family who established the area's first farm in 1647 and whose memory is also enshrined, albeit with a different spelling, in the name of Brooklyn's Ditmas Park. The Ditmars name in Queens, in any case, is hardly as evocative as that of the handsome arc of iron—the Hell Gate Bridge—that dominates its views and stands as an exemplar of how fortuitously, sometimes, the translation of Dutch names into English ones worked out: The Dutch term for where the East River meets Long Island Sound, Hellgat, meant "beautiful strait," but its English translation was perhaps more apt for a passage whose submerged rocks, beneath treacherous currents, wrecked a lot of ships before they were dynamited to mud in 1885. Nowadays, the neighborhood by Hell Gate is home to humans from even more places than appeared in Raymond Lee Ditmars's bestselling book from 1910, *Reptiles of the World,* which helped lots of American kids learn world geography.

Astoria's Greeks have now been joined by Egyptians and Yemenis and other Arabic speakers from the Middle East; by Brazilians and Bangladeshis and Taiwanese; by Maltese and by Mexicans, too, like the marvelous mason from Puebla, Manuel, who told me recently that, although his kids were still struggling to learn English, they were going to school with children of parents from Salonika or Crete and thus now had, to his wonderment, learned to speak Greek. These new Astorians are now also being joined, naturally, by deal-hunting yuppies fleeing Brooklyn. But theirs remains one of New York's best neighborhoods for pondering how and why and when new arrivals to America count as American, and who decides.

These aren't new questions in a country brought into being by fifty-six people who all happened to be white men of English or Irish descent, and where humans of other descriptions have often not been accorded, to put it gently, the rights implied by truths those fifty-six white men proclaimed self-evident. But they are questions that perhaps take on an extra-vivid hue when pondering, as one walks Astoria's blocks, the millions of poor beavers who died to make the Astors rich or what exactly the bearded men talking jovial shit in Arabic, outside the Egyptian coffee shops now lining Steinway Street, are discussing as they puff date-sweetened tobacco from tall water pipes. And there's nowhere for bringing those implications home—in my personal geography of New York greasy spoons, anyway—like the Bel Aire Diner, just off Broadway at 31-91 21st Street.

With its blue pleather booths and book-thick menu laminated in plastic, the Bel Aire is a fine specimen of a dying American breed. Twenty years ago, there were as many diners in New York as the Bel Aire has found ways—some 1,200, in that voluminous menu—to combine eggs and bacon and bread products and beef into discrete dishes. Nowadays, there are a third as many. In New

York, rising rents have imperiled this most American genre of eatery. Diners have for a century now been businesses whose margins depend on volume and speed—on running a full-service restaurant where prices are low and portions large and the aim is to move you out the door in forty minutes or less, but where servers treat you like royalty, or at least call you "hon" as they refill your coffee. Maintaining those margins in a city where commercial rents can now cost $20,000 or $30,000 or more a month, even in once-plebeian zones outside Manhattan, isn't easy. Thirty grand is a lot of omelets. But stalwarts like the Bel Aire, just down 21st Street from where my father-in-law grew up on a block that once was Jewish but isn't now, endure as institutions that feel a lot more democratic, a lot of the time, than American democracy. And they persist as symbols, too, of the kind of ethnic alchemy that the American experiment has also long wrought.

Or so it felt to me, anyway, one morning at the Bel Aire, when I asked the place's proprietor a question that many New Yorkers have perhaps pondered but not answered: Why is it that every diner in New York is owned by Greeks? The answer doesn't lie in some demotic attachment to the *demos* or a national talent for flipping burgers. It lies, as the Bel Aire's proprietor told me, in the mug of coffee my waitress had just warmed up. And in the story of how a Greek immigrant named John Vassilaros, in the 1920s, built a coffee-wholesaling business that became *the* supplier of a distinctive light-roast java, much easier to imbibe in bulk than the inky stuff now dispensed at Starbucks, to lunch counters across New York. Vassilaros's genius was to use his profits to help his striving countrymen, who were then much more likely to be employed in city restaurants as dishwashers or cooks, to start running them. Vassilaros helped hundreds of Greeks, both local veterans of the industry and new arrivals fleeing war, to buy diners where they agreed, in exchange, to only ever serve Vassilaros & Sons Coffee.

Such are the roots of the Greek dominance of New York's diners and of the lasting success of Vassilaros's company, which is now run by his great-grandkids. Headquartered in a 25,000-square-foot factory near LaGuardia Airport, they sell enough coffee—a mix of beans from Brazil and Colombia, roasted for nine minutes in 522-pound batches—to fill five million cups a week. It's a lovely story that's been written up elsewhere. You should read about it, if you're interested. But in the meantime, if you happen to find yourself in Astoria some morning or late night, stop in at the Bel Aire—like all diners worth their sea salt, it's open twenty-four hours— for some scrambled eggs with black olives and pita. Look out for the balding man by the register, who's manned his post there, often for up to sixteen hours a day, for the past quarter-century. And then ask Argyris "Archie" Dellaportas, who landed in Astoria from Cephalonia in 1972 and then saved up to buy the Bel Aire, to regale you with tales from his business. Just don't ask him to reveal the names of his most prized employees. It's not that Archie doesn't value his crack team of line cooks, and a pair of brothers from Oaxaca who bake all his bread on the premises. On the contrary: He doesn't want anyone to steal them away in this city where Mexicans, as Greeks did decades ago, dominate restaurant kitchens of all kinds. When and whether this newer group soon gains its own John Vassilaros, to help move them out of New York's kitchens and into another niche, remains to be seen. But just remember, after Archie doesn't discuss any of this with you, that your all-American meal in this enterprise run by a man from Cephalonia was prepared by others from Culiacán. *Hamilton* may have made this insight a hit, but it's not new: In America, it's immigrants who get the job done.

5.

LEAVING SHORE:
CITY OF ISLANDS

Shooters Island: I always did want to go. Both because of its name and because of where it's at. In the Kill Van Kull between New Jersey and Staten Island, Shooters is the flat green-brown cake you glimpse to your right when rolling south over the Bayonne Bridge (or to starboard if you're a mariner ambling the deck of one of the huge Panamax freighters that float under the bridge, each day, to offload containers of cars by Newark Bay). Like many of New York's smaller islands, Shooters boasts a colorful human history. It got its name from British colonists who used it as a hunting reserve, before it served as a haven for Revolutionary spies in George Washington's day, and then for major shipyards and an oil refinery in Woodrow Wilson's. But like many such places in New York's waters, it's now a place where humans aren't allowed. Sumac and creepers poke through its industrial ruins; listing skeletons of old boats creak offshore. Since Shooters was turned into a bird sanctuary run by the Parks Department a few decades back, its avian population has grown to include several dozen nesting pairs of glossy ibises, black-crowned herons, and snowy egrets.

New York is a city of islands. Manhattan is an island. So, of course, is Staten Island. Queens and Brooklyn may be claimed by the city, but they're also Long Island's nub. Only one of Gotham's boroughs—the Bronx—is actually linked by land to North America. And two small islands in New York Harbor have served as enduring symbols of two values sacred to the city—arrival and aspiration—that still play an outsized role in shaping both how America imagines New York and how New York sees itself. When the government of the young United States commandeered two blots of silt in the tidal flats off Jersey City, its imagined use for the islands, then named Bedloe's and Ellis for their colonial owners, was strictly military. But then in 1886, the government of France gifted the United States a humongous copper statue to hail its liberty's centennial a decade before. The statue's recipients decided to place it on Bedloe's—later Liberty—Island, and to turn nearby Ellis Island into the place where some twelve million immigrants from over the ocean, between 1892 and 1954, became Americans. Which is how these two islands came to embody to many, especially those who glimpsed Ms. Liberty's torch and crown as their ships neared Ellis's docks, the sentiment of a famous poem stuck to her base in 1903.

Those lines by Emma Lazarus voiced America's

openness to the planet's tired and poor and "huddled masses yearning to breathe free"; they welcomed cast-offs from the Old World who were often destined, in the New, to land in city tenements where "breathe free" was a mean joke. But islands didn't cease to matter in the minds of those new New Yorkers once they departed Ellis Island for Brooklyn or the Lower East Side. The place they learned to venture to for air and fun in the summertime was an island—Coney Island—that is not one (and was joined to Brooklyn, in the twenties, by the plugging up of Coney Island Creek). The place where those strivers in the city ended up, if they didn't manage to ascend from its slums but instead landed in its gutters, was an island, too—the "damnation island" in the East River that became home to the city's main prison, poorhouse, and insane asylum (it's named Roosevelt Island today). And from the nineteenth century to today, there's been no sadder end to which a New York life can come than to see its earthly remains shipped to Hart Island, off the Bronx. This is where upward of a million indigent or unclaimed New Yorkers have been laid to rest in mass graves dug by inmates from an island off Queens—Rikers—that's served since the Depression as the city's jail.

The geography of New York's smaller islands contains vital chapters in the city's larger social history, and key nodes in its imagination now. Each of the city's boroughs includes in its territory, floating in Jamaica Bay or off the Bronx or in Staten Island's Arthur Kill, dozens of islets and islands that give charts of its waters the look of Earthsea or the Aegean. These islands, by their mere names and presence, have always enthralled map geeks. But they've also enacted a special pull for intrepid urbanists and birders. Because Shooters Island is hardly alone, among what might be called the out islands of New York, in combining two elements to which members of those odd tribes thrill: the remains of bygone industry or human habitation, and a new efflorescence of wildlife that recalls their ecology's prehuman roots. These portals to the city's past also suggest, in their eerie colonies of wading birds and ruined buildings, a posthuman future. And many of them have names—from Rat to Ruffle to Mau Mau to the pair called Brother—that compose a suggestive poetry to match.

ISLANDS HAVE LONG LODGED in our minds, and featured in our literature, as places to be marooned or transformed; as paradises or prisons; as points for embarkation or arrival. "Islands are our planet's poems," observed the writer Robert Sullivan, a connoisseur of the islands of New York. "Tight, circumscribed, they are other, defined against the landmass from which they broke or the sea from which they emerged." And whether glimpsed by explorers in olden days or by city dwellers peering over the rails, today, of its ferries or bridges, New York's islands have a way of becoming symbols—of liberty or purgatory or welfare or worse. It's no surprise that lots of them have evocative names. And it's telling of much about not merely the city's history but its collective psychology to trace the evolution of its islands' labels across the centuries since three of them near a place the Hackensack called Communipaw ("landing place by the river") were dubbed Oester Eilanden ("oyster islands") by the Dutch.

The Oester Eiland that was renamed Bedloe's after its first English buyer in 1667 retained that name despite a later owner who tried, in the mid-1700s and when seeking a long-term tenant for this place "from where any quantity of pickled oysters may be transported," as that owner's advertisement put it, to dub the place Love Island instead. It's a pity, for writers of doggerel and of newspaper headlines anyway, that this name didn't stick: They would have had fun heralding the island's later transition, from Love to Liberty. But it's often hard to know why some colloquial names stick and some don't—especially when a place is transformed beyond recognition from the aspect that named it. That's the case with the green picnic area, in Liberty State Park, that's now got the name of the third Oester Eiland in these parts: Black Tom.

In colonial days Black Tom was little more than a large and jagged rock, evidently dark in complexion. Why English seamen of yore liked calling menacing rocks "Tom" is unclear. But this was indeed their habit. Black Tom has a fraternal twin, off the Bronx in Eastchester Bay: It's a sub-marine rock, called Big Tom, whose top sometimes isn't visible even at low tide but which is still labeled on Google Maps. For Black Tom's part, he became a more substantial proposition when some wise minds moved to soften his edges, in the 1880s, by dumping bargefuls of gravel around them. As Ellis Island would also be after its area was expanded with rubble from the digging of the city's subways, the new and bigger Black Tom was linked to New Jersey by causeway. It came to comprise twenty-five acres of depots and piers and train tracks, which were used by munitions makers, during World War I, to sell arms to the French and English— until a pair of German secret agents attached some pencil bombs to two million pounds of glycerin one night in 1916 and lit the fuse. The resulting blast, measuring 5.5 on the Richter scale, shattered windows as far away as Times Square. It also liquefied much of Black Tom into sludge. Its remaining landfill acreage was connected to the mainland and now supports that picnic area in Liberty State Park. But Black Tom's story stands as an allegory for the era when New York's harbor was becoming the busiest in the world, and when many of its islands, to meet the needs of commerce or state, were altered or disappeared or made from nothing.

Two of the latter breed of island—the kind made by men—resemble deserted hexagons beneath the Verrazzano Bridge. There, by where captains from the Sandy Hook Pilots Association still guide every large ship that arrives in New York through its Narrows, these hexagons were created in the 1870s by dumping fill onto shoals. They're "quarantine islands," built for immigrants known or suspected to be infected with cholera or yellow fever. The larger of the two, Hoffman Island, was named for a prominent politician of the day: It housed patients merely detained for observation. The smaller one, named Swinburne Island after a celebrated Civil War surgeon, was for the acutely sick: Its grim four acres of gravel were outfitted with both a hospital and an at-the-ready crematory for poor souls who crossed the sea to reach America but perished here before reaching shore. Today both Hoffman and Swinburne are uninhabited by humans, but prized by lovers of urban lore about porn flicks shot amid their hospitals' ruins in the 1970s, and by nature lovers who thrill at glimpsing the whiskered harbor seals here who've returned to New York after a century's absence and love sunning their backs on Swinburne's rocks.

One island that wasn't made from scratch but substantially altered, in the early twentieth century, looms green and lovely off the Battery in lower Manhattan. Governors Island is 172 acres of old forts and breezy greenspace, now open to the public; it's reachable by ferry in the summer. Back when it was a third of its current size and covered in chestnut trees, the Lenape knew it as Paggank—"nut island." That native place-name became a Dutch one— Noten Eylandt—which the English Anglicized to Nutten Island before moving, in 1698, to reserve the island for their colonial governor. When the victors in the Revolutionary War took over what was by 1783 known as Governor's Island, they effected what must be the subtlest but most piquant transition from past to present tense in the history of New York naming. They removed the apostrophe in "Governor's" to turn the old possessive into a new name—Governors Island—that evoked colonial administrators who owned it once but didn't anymore.

The island's new American owners built star-shaped Fort Jay on its old central knoll and then the cylinder-shaped castle to its northwest, Fort William, whose casemate cannons were finished in time to be ready to repel an attack by the Brits during the War of 1812 that never came. A century later, bits of bedrock blasted from beneath Lexington Avenue by the IRT were used to more than double the island's size. The Army built an airstrip and barracks and training grounds that got much use during World War II and that later became the Coast Guard's. The island remained in federal hands until 1996, when it was returned to New York. It then moldered for a decade, during which state and city agencies and developers with dollar signs for eyes argued over proposals like Mayor Rudy Giuliani's hope that Governors be turned over to casino hotels. But now it's emerged as a marvelously unfinished public park that can't be beat, on a summer Sunday, for riding a bike past old forts and new pieces of public art and more unexpected layers in the urban machine—like the round edifice off its northeast shoulder that looks like a cross between a fort and a sculpture, but is in fact a mighty vent that pulls carbon monoxide up from the Brooklyn-Battery Tunnel below to prevent motorists from choking on their own exhaust. Around a grassy lawn here that's shaded with ancient oaks and ringed by dilapidated officers' homes like the one where I spent a great summer on an arts residency, the air is anything but poisonous. Especially when the old Admiral's House is turned into the American Indian Community House, on weekends, and members of New York's Silvercloud drummers beat a big circular drum on its portico and sing songs to recall their Lenape kin who called this place Paggank.

IT IS HARD TO conjure a more palpable tableau than that one for pondering the sounds and traces of history that can feel—on islands everywhere—closer to the surface. But if you don't have a ferry of your own, you can reach Governors Island only when it's running. At other times, and for those with access not to a boat but to wheels and who prefer their brushes with history to feel less overt, the island I'd most commend for such musings now isn't an island at all. To get there you roll across Brooklyn all the way to where Flatbush Avenue extends out over Jamaica Bay—but then be sure to pull over, before you climb the Marine Parkway–Gil Hodges Memorial Bridge to the Rockaways, by the roadway's right edge. Though the land you're standing on has been connected to Brooklyn with fill since the 1920s, it still has a name—Barren Island—from when it wasn't. Hacking through a tangle of bayberry here, you'll emerge onto the shore of a place whose own moniker—Dead Horse Bay—derives from one of the notorious uses to which Barren Island was once put.

That use dates from when the city's streets teemed not with taxis, but buggies and carts: This is where the horses that pulled them were brought by scow, after they expired, to be turned into glue. Alongside its horse-rendering plants, Barren Island was also home to a big landfill, and another stinky industry: several firms whose business was boiling dead fish and bat guano into fertilizer. "Hundreds of thousands have had an olfactory introduction to Barren Island," reported the *New York Times* in 1890, "though few have ever visited it." The island's English name, in stories like that one, seemed apt to its aspect. But it's actually an Anglicization of what some old Dutchman, apparently having spotted some large fauna here that's no longer common to Brooklyn, dubbed Beeren Eylandt ("bear island"). Those who did visit Barren Island by rowboat or scow found a tight-knit community of outcasts—Black immigrants from down south and white ones from Italy or the Rhine—who worked in its plants and fed their families with clams and stripers pulled from parts of the bay not also swimming, or so one hopes, with offal.

When Barren Island's putrescent industries were shuttered, residents and real estate agents in now nicer-smelling nearby neighborhoods like Flatlands and Broad Channel rejoiced. The bargefuls of rubble used to connect it to the mainland in the twenties enabled the building of New York's first municipal airstrip, Floyd Bennett Field. But it was a further attempt to expand what should perhaps now have been termed, by rights, the Barren Peninsula—master planner Robert Moses's doomed stab in the 1950s at expanding its acreage to the west by covering a big dump's worth of garbage with nothing but topsoil—that gave Dead Horse Bay its chief distinction now. The tides' reaction to Moses's plan was predictable: They stripped away the dirt to leave, poking from the sand, a layered cake of the sort of refuse that doesn't biodegrade. Which is why and how a beach once known for its horse bones is now famed, among amateur city archaeologists and kayakers, for the glinting carpet of thick-glassed bottles—brown or blue or clear, whole or in parts—that emerge here at low tide, their embossed-in-glass names signaling whether they once contained aspirin or bleach or Yuengling beer.

Glass Bottle Beach, Barren Island, Dead Horse Bay—the sequence of names sounds like a series of plot points in a fantastical novel about pirates. But they also label a real place that can't be beat, as discerning scavengers know, for hunting urban treasure that's not limited to objects. The last time I was there, a pair of art students were yanking on what looked like a thick black fishing line. It was actually a cord to whose end was attached an underwater microphone, they said, with which they were capturing the tinkling sound of glass being massaged by waves over rocks.

FROM WHERE I STOOD talking with those art students, the great marsh-dotted expanse of the bay that the Canarsee called Equendito ("broken lands"), and which is now named for Queens' county seat, spread in all directions. Jamaica Bay is the westernmost of the tidal lagoons that line Long Island's southern shore. It's a mecca for migrating birds—fully twenty percent of North America's avian species alight here each year—that was once New York City's chief destination for waste. A nine-thousand-acre swimming pool of salt marsh and grassy islands, it has also again become a place, since it became protected parkland in 1973, where one can ogle a nesting osprey from a canoe as bluefish bump your paddle. But this is also among the parts of New York's map, at least in terms of how the contours of its coastline and islands have changed, that humans have altered most—not least by building a new airport by its eastern edge, in 1948, that's a whole lot bigger than Floyd Bennett Field. When this new airport opened, it was named for a golf course on whose grounds it was partly built. According to George Stewart, the name Idlewild was "an American variant of 'Idyllwild,' a commendatory name for a resort, suggesting vacation and unspoiled nature." According to others, it's a neologism that entered English usage only thanks to *Anne of Green Gables,* the beloved Victorian novel for young adults published in 1908. Either way, the name of what's now New York's busiest port of entry was changed after the murder, in 1963, of a beloved president. Now John F. Kennedy is what we call this piece of infrastructure that's allowed millions of people to see Jamaica Bay, though most don't know what they're looking at, from above.

One pleasure of examining a map of the islets and pools those plane passengers gaze down upon is the wealth of names—on modern charts of the bay as much as on old ones—whose provenance is lost. Among the ones coined by long-ago oystermen and boaters that are with us still but whose meaning is not are marshes named Old Swale and Elders Point and JoCo. Another's called the Pumpkin Patch. The Raunt, a place-name that's now attached to little more than a silty channel, recalls a stop on the old railroad built in 1880 to cross the bay—saloons and fishing clubs stood on stilts by its trestle—to the Rockaways. Jamaica Bay's got an island called Plumb and one called Ruffle Bar. It also has several whose names—Grass Hassock, Winhole Hassock, Rulers Bar Hassock—employ an old English term for a tuft of grass. There are places here called Yellow Bar, Black Bar, and Black Bank. Down by Silver Hole Marsh, the Vernam Barbadoes Peninsula juts between two inlets called Barbadoes (named for the Caribbean island) and Vernam (named for a nineteenth-century entrepreneur, Remington Vernam, who opened the Rockaways' first destination hotel). The nearby neighborhoods of Arverne and Arverne-by-the-Sea were named by Vernam's wife: She thought the way her husband signed his checks, as R. Vernam, "had a nice French sound." She riffed on that sound to attach it to developments her husband built on a peninsula whose dunes became a popular destination for the hundreds of thousands of beach-seeking New Yorkers who were, by the last century's turn, riding the train past the Raunt to get here in summer.

That train line's terminus wasn't far from the broad beach that in 1914 became what must be one of the world's only major public parks named for a documentary photographer: Jacob Riis Park. Holiday makers here, whether hailing from the Manhattan tenements Riis photographed or the Tammany Hall machine that controlled them, could in the late nineteenth century venture even farther south by boat. Their destination was a mile-long sandbar that emerged from the waves around the time of the Civil War and was built up, in ensuing years, with its own seaside saloons and inns. It was known as Hog Island not because it was home to pigs, but because its profile's curving aspect was reminiscent, to some, of a porcine spine—at least until a big hurricane overswept its drinking spots, in 1893, with thirty-foot waves. Hog Island disappeared completely a few years later, thanks to erosion and the same shifting currents that birthed it.

Jamaica Bay's marsh islands, in more recent times,

have also been disappearing. Decreased pollution and the bay's protected status have seen the return of many fish and also unique species like the diamondback terrapin turtles now spotted, on occasion, crossing runways at JFK. But nearby sewage treatment plants, scientists say, are still pumping too much nitrogen into the bay. The nitrogen has joined with rising seas to make salt marshes, and the marine and other life-forms that both depend on them and help them thrive continue to shrink. Some of the bay's islands that persist, like Canarsie Pol, have names—"pol" is an Old Dutch term for an island that's man-made—that give clues as to why they survived. Also man-made are Subway Island, here—its land was dredged from the muck to let the A train reach Arverne—and another island off the bay's western edge in Gerritsen Creek. This island was plunked there with a mix of garbage and fill in 1917, and its official name is still the one it was given then—White Island—to honor the Gilded Age landowner who donated what's now Marine Park to the city. But since the 1960s it's been more commonly known as Mau Mau.

How and why this deserted patch of cordgrass came to be named, or seems to have been named, for an African uprising against colonial rule in Kenya remains mysterious. So does the source, as it happens, of the name of Kenya's Mau Mau rebellion (whose protagonists' tag is variously said to be a reappropriated British slur for Kenya's Kikuyu people, a bastardization of a Kikuyu phrase for "our grandfathers," or an anagram of a Swahili phrase meaning "get out, get out"). But whatever those rebels' name's source, their bloody bravery was much in the news in the 1950s: It inspired a notorious Puerto Rican street gang in Brooklyn to call themselves Mau Maus. It's unclear whether their inspiration, or some other root, is behind the same tag being attached to this garbage island that became a golf course and is now left to its birds. But what's not unclear is why a plurality of residents of nearby neighborhoods, not to mention the artsy hipsters from elsewhere in Brooklyn who've staged a ritualistic "Battle for Mau Mau Island" on its beaches, prefer the phrase "Mau Mau" to "White."

Rituals and islands, to say nothing of islands and artists, have long gone together. Where the materiel employed by participants in the Battle for Mau Mau Island include wooden swords and inflatable dinghies, other islands in Jamaica Bay are today littered with the shells of coconuts: the remnants of Hindu ceremonies, performed at the bay's edge by residents of nearby neighborhoods full of working-class immigrants.

The city artist who has made these islands more central to his work than any other in recent years has found several other equally evocative ways to animate their import. Duke Riley runs a tattoo parlor when he's not paddling out to Ruffle Bar for fun or making scrimshaw-style murals of sea scenes and seals for leading museums. Among the other ways he's fed his passion for New York's maritime past at its margins is by opening a site-specific temporary speakeasy by Dead Horse Bay, which he called the Dead Horse Inn and where he sold crabs for a nickel; by convincing the Queens Museum to let him add handmade models of Hoffman and Swinburne Islands to its famous scale model of the city, the Panorama; and by crafting a wooden one-man submarine, modeled on a similar vessel used during the Revolutionary War to ambush British ships here, which he launched into the Buttermilk Channel to recall this history by "attacking" the *Queen Mary 2* (and to attract the attention, in the event, of Coast Guardsmen who arrested him before he could get near it). In 2016, Duke staged a luminous tribute involving a huge flock of carrier pigeons with LED lights strapped to their legs, which he released from the Brooklyn Navy Yard to hail these birds' long-vital role in naval communications.

But it was another stunt that landed Riley in cuffs on a Coast Guard cutter, though it also succeeded in teaching denizens of the city's art world, anyway, about Manhattan's smallest island. This thirty-yard-long clump of rocks in the East River is an outpost for cormorants, just offshore of the United Nations headquarters by East 42nd Street. Its official name is Belmont Island and it was created by the construction of a subway tunnel directly beneath it, whose construction was begun in the 1890s by William Steinway: The piano magnate sought to connect Manhattan via trolley to Steinway Village in Queens. The resulting island was officially named, after the opening in 1907 of a tunnel through which the 7 train now runs, for the financier who enabled its completion after Steinway's death, August Belmont. But the island's prominent place in vistas enjoyed by representatives to the UN and employees of that organization, whose high modernist home was opened nearby in 1953, has made it a magnet for other ideas and causes. Among these were the activists who occupied the island to protest Leonid Brezhnev in 1972 and gave it the symbolic name of Soviet Jewry Freedom Island. That name didn't stick. But it was in a related spirit that members of a group called Peace Meditation at the United Nations, a few years later, leased Belmont Island from the State of New York and announced that, at the urging of their guru Sri Chinmoy, they would be renaming the island for a late secretary-general of the UN, U Thant, a Burmese diplomat whose "world-harmony role" they esteemed. Which is how and why it was that in 2004, when Duke Riley paddled here from Brooklyn under cover of night and during a Republican National Convention that put the city on lockdown, he found some metal scaffolding placed here by its Buddhist makers to hold a sign announcing the island's new name. The flag Riley hung on this scaffolding to declare U Thant Island a sovereign nation was twenty-one feet long and depicted two electric eels that looked to be gazing north, during the twenty minutes or so they were in place, toward Roosevelt Island.

. . .

THAT TWO-MILE BAND of schist running up Manhattan's east side is known today for apartment buildings favored by diplomats, a cable car loved by Spider-Man, and a Louis Kahn–designed monument, by its southern tip, to the Roosevelt for whom this island was named in 1973 (Franklin, not Teddy). Known before that as Welfare Island, it wasn't a place that New Yorkers then wanted to come to: The Queensboro Bridge was built to fly over it, in 1909, for a reason. Deeper in the past, the Lenape called it Minnehanonck ("long island"), and the Dutch dubbed it Varkens Eylandt ("hog island"), before it was acquired around 1700 by an Englishman whose name was still attached to it when the island, then called Blackwell's, became home in 1839 to the New York City Lunatic Asylum. That city institution was soon joined by several others—its main prison for hardened criminals, its workhouse for pettier ones, and its main charity hospital for the poor—after which Blackwell's Island became known as Welfare Island. But its more popular name, among the "rounders" who spent years being shuffled among its scary buildings in the late 1800s, was "damnation island": Nearly one in ten New Yorkers, at a time when any random pharmacist or cop could have a poor Irish girl or mouthy street urchin committed, came here to die or to go crazy. As the journalist Nellie Bly narrated in *Ten Days in a Mad-house,* her famous 1887 account of getting herself sent on purpose to this island, it was "a human rat trap . . . easy to get in, but once there it is impossible to get out."

The two now-conjoined islands off Roosevelt's upper tip—Wards and Randall's—were also home, during New York's Dickensian era, to damnation island facilities for its impoverished and ill. But the weight of the past, on these two park islands that anchor the Triborough Bridge and are now used for high school sports and art fairs, hasn't required changing their labels: The surnames of the old Englishmen who owned them long ago (and whose islands were joined to each other with fill in the sixties) still work fine. The same is true of another, smaller pair that sit northeast of where Wards and Randall's guard the Hell Gate, off Hunts Point in the Bronx. North Brother and South Brother Island got their English names, like their Dutch one before it—De Gesellen ("the companions")—for their proximity and resemblance. Over the years, they've been put to many uses. One of these is captured in some excellent photographs that hang in the East Village at McSorley's Old Ale House, as Joseph Mitchell reported long ago and I can affirm is still so, of jolly outings to North Brother, the larger of the pair, once undertaken by The Honorable John McSorley Pickle, Beefsteak, Baseball Nine, and Chowder Club. Now North Brother is perhaps best known for other photos: images of a crumbling hospital here—once used for quarantined sufferers of smallpox and typhus—that will pop right up if you hunt the Internet for "ruin porn." Today the Brothers, officially left to their birds, are home to the city's largest colony of black-crowned night herons. But the scant kayakers and birders who make it here to see them, if few others, can best appreciate the provenance of the islands' names when approaching them by water. The same's true as they float past New York's last and largest island of the damned— Rikers—to reach the many rocky islets of Pelham Bay. Along this coast of New York that angles toward New England, many islands' names, though their roots are much debated, seem to evoke how they look on maps or from across the water.

The Blauzes, for example, are a pair of stony domes that local fishermen call "the blue breasts," but whose official name is thought to derive either from the Old English "blazer," meaning "marker," or the Dutch "de blautjes," for "little blue ones." The Chimney Sweeps, another duo rising from the reef, are said to have reminded long-ago boatmen either of an old-fashioned tool for scrubbing flues or of, well, two dingy rocks in need of cleaning. You might think Rat Island is named for vermin. Actually, it's named—according, anyway, to the Swiss guy who now owns it and placed a statue of William Tell on its rocks— for the rattles once used here to warn off ships. The name of High Island, which is reachable at low tide on foot but off-limits to visitors, long predates its current use, but that use is apt: The island's primary feature has for decades been the high AM radio tower from whence the voices of squawking Mets fans and talk jocks on WFAN and WCBS, respectively, energize commuters. The prize for most intriguingly named islands in this part of the city may go to a pair called Nonations. These tiny islets' tags—East Nonations and West Nonations—evoke the vexed role that islands have played in conflicts over sovereignty since long before the era of Duke Riley and Sri Chinmoy. The most plausible explanation of the name is that the English and Dutch both deemed them of such little worth that neither claimed them. But you've got to love those who contend, *pace* that theory, that the name is actually a typo—that it was in fact coined by a lover of English grammar whose intent, perhaps struck by the islands' resemblance to ellipses or asterisks signaling footnotes, was to dub them "Notations."

The biggest and best-known island in this region of the city is the only one you can reach by car. Before you get to City Island, you exit the Bruckner Expressway, just before the Bruckner exits the Bronx, and roll through a big greensward at the city's northeast edge—Pelham Bay Park—that's beloved by bathers and barbecuers who flock here, in the summer, to hang out on Orchard Beach. That great half-ring of sand was built in 1934 by Robert Moses, who floated millions of tons of sand from the Rockaways and joined three nearby islands—Twin Islands (there were two of them) and Hunter Island (once used for hunting)—to Rodman's Neck, as the peninsula the park occupies is called, to create the Bronx's only public beach.

But to reach the island here that Moses didn't touch, you continue on toward the NYPD firing range that's been disturbing the peace here for decades. You follow signs to a place whose name sounds like it sprang from the brain of Robert Moses, but in fact dates from 1761. That's when an enterprising man named Benjamin Palmer bought a rocky mile-and-a-half-long spray of rock off Rodman's Neck and dubbed it New City Island.

PALMER'S NEW PROPERTY WAS called Minneford's Island at the time: It was a part of the larger parcel that Thomas Pell acquired from the Siwanoy sachem, Minneford, a century before. Palmer's vision for the place, which was home to only a few hearty farmers and oystermen, was to build a seaport here to rival Manhattan. His island did thrive as a home to shipwrights who still make world-class yachts in its yards, but it never became a commercial center of the sort the word "city" implies. One nonetheless wonders if its name (which lost its "new" at some point) may have played at least a subconscious role in its citizens' vote to have their island, which until 1896 was part of Pelham, in Westchester County, become a part of New York City instead.

Also key to that decision was a promise from politicians in faraway Manhattan. They told City Islanders that if they defected from Westchester for New York City, the Department of Transportation would build them a bridge to the Bronx. Thus was City Island made a part of greater Gotham in 1898 and joined to its mainland by a permanent link that's now jammed, on summer days, with cars and livery cabs inching onto City Island Avenue. Up and down the island's main drag, people tumble from those cars into one of the thirty seafood restaurants that sling frozen drinks and crab legs and fried shrimp by the pound and have become City Island's raison d'être (at least to other Bronxites).

These restaurants recall the maritime past of a one-time fishing village whose nickname for its native-born is still "clamdiggers" (non-natives are called "musselsuckers"), but whose urban present is underscored by the truth that none of its eateries, today, serves any food from the water they overlook. Shellfish from any of greater New York's waters were long ago deemed unsafe, on account of the PCBs absorbed in their flesh, by the state Department of Health. Every lobster or fried clam dished up at Johnny's Reef or the City Island Lobster House gets here by the same route those joints' patrons do: by crossing the causeway, on a truck. But this hardly matters to the loyal diners who hang a quick left off the bridge to head toward the Lobster House's beckoning red roof, which was adorned until 2012 with a giant lobster that the place's owner, Jojo Mandarino, called Larry.

Sadly, Larry the Lobster was badly damaged in Superstorm Sandy ("We had to chop him up," Manzarano told the *Bronx Times*), and he's now left his perch above a parking lot that smells of the sea and of garlic. But the free garlic bread inside is delicious. And so is the general ambience at a place where happy patrons in plastic bibs—whether couples celebrating anniversaries, hustlers a big score, families a niece's graduation or a patriarch's birthday—tuck into the sort of portions, washed down with boozy glasses of City Island Iced Tea ("watch out!" the menu warns), that you'd never find at a place catering to the rich.

Establishments like the Lobster House are worthy destinations in themselves. But among the other reasons that City Island is worth a visit are the fiberglass boats available for rent here at Jack's Bait & Tackle. They can be had for $70 a day, as indicated by a list of offerings above the register at Jack's that also includes jars of sandworms and nightcrawlers. These vessels are equipped with little 8-horsepower motors and beloved by amateur casters. But they're also great for chugging around the bay to inspect the Devil's Stepping Stones, which skip off toward Great Neck, and a more solitary rock named, for unclear reasons, Cuban Ledge (theories range from commemoration of the explosion of the USS *Maine* in Havana in 1898 to the rock's alleged resemblance to a Cuban cigar). But these boats won't work for getting you to the bigger landmass, dotted with abandoned buildings, that is visible to City Island's east. When I asked one of the guys at Jack's what would happen if I successfully navigated the shoals there to reach Hart Island's shore, he gave me a look reserved, it seemed, for dumb-ass musselsuckers: "They'll lock you up real quick."

Presumably he meant officers from the Department of Corrections, who've held jurisdiction over Hart Island since the 1950s and patrol its perimeter by boat. Here at "the world's largest taxpayer-funded cemetery," inmates from Rikers have for decades done the grim work of interring New York's luckless dead. "Potter's fields" like Hart take their name from the biblical plot of clay where Judas lay. New York has had several. Washington Square Park was one, once upon a time. So was Bryant Park, by the public library. Before Hart Island became the city's main destination for unclaimed bodies, Randall's Island was. But then the city bought this place whose name is said to derive either from a colonial cartographer who was struck by its organlike shape (and thus dubbed it "Heart Island") or from the fact that it was once home to lots of male deer the English called "harts." In the early 1800s, its bucolic acreage hosted picnickers and bare-knuckle boxing bouts. During the Civil War, it served as both a prison for Confederate POWs and a training camp for U.S. Colored Troops. But then the city bought Hart in 1868 and reserved half of its hundred-odd acres for a new municipal graveyard for the fast-growing metropolis. By the time Jacob Riis visited Hart in 1890, to photograph the place where many of the immigrant poor he photographed on the Lower East Side ended up, Hart's potter's field was serving as a final home, Riis estimated, for a similar percentage of New Yorkers—one in ten—as were damned to Blackwell's while they were alive.

Between that era and today, Hart's loamy dirt has received the remains of perhaps a million souls. Placed in pine boxes and then stacked three and four deep in wide trenches, the dead here are still handled in the same way you can see in Riis's photos from the nineteenth century, or in an upsetting video that's findable on YouTube, shot in 1978 by a local news crew that somehow convinced the DOC to let them film workmen from Rikers tossing around infant-sized caskets like footballs. Until shockingly recently, little was publicly known about who was buried at Hart and in which plot. The closest that even relatives of the deceased could get was City Island's eastern edge, from whence one can glimpse, alongside the spooky ruins of a psychiatric hospital also once located here, a couple fields dotted with wooden posts, painted white. With each of those posts signifying a trench in which 150 adults or 1,000 babies were interred, Hart's dead have ranged from the unhoused and stillborn to some of New York's first victims of AIDS. Among those who were buried here in 1985, before AIDS was well understood and beneath an extra fourteen feet of soil, was the trans woman Rachel Humphreys, whose courage and charms inspired her lover in the seventies, Lou Reed, to write "Coney Island Baby." The city's first baby to die of the disease is here, too. She or he now occupies the only individual grave on the island. Beneath a figure of a praying cherub, its granite marker reads "SC [special child] B1 [Baby 1] 1985."

We know these things, along with much of what's now been made publicly available about the island, thanks to an artist named Melinda Hunt. In the 1990s, Hunt and the photographer Joel Sternfeld gained permission from the DOC to follow in Jacob Riis's footsteps and document Hart's graves for a book. She also founded the Hart Island Project, an art endeavor in the public interest whose fruits now include a remarkable website that not only allows users to find information, pulled from city records obtained by Hunt with the help of the state's Freedom of Information Law, about where and when the dead here from recent decades were buried. It also allows them to add biographical and other information to the often-sparse details ("Helen Santiago, August 20, 2009") those records contain. A few years ago, the Hart Island Project's years-long campaign to get the city to allow relatives of the dead to come and pay their respects, on regularly scheduled visits arranged by the DOC, finally prevailed.

The Hart Island Project was also behind a more recent and radical landmark in Hart's evolution. In December 2019, not long after the City Council voted to pursue closing the Rikers Island jail, the same body moved to turn over control of Hart Island from the DOC to the Parks Department. This change entails an eventual phasing out of the use of its potter's field, and for regular ferry service to the island, along with facilities for those wishing to visit. On the day the mayor signed these intents into law, his pen's movement was met with whoops and cheers from watching members of the Hart Island Project, and a broad smile from the bespectacled woman—Melinda Hunt—who beamed over his shoulder.

Little did either Melinda Hunt or the mayor know that Hart would soon be in the news for sadder reasons. Nor did I, when I contacted the DOC that winter to reserve a spot on the once-monthly sailing to Hart they'd just begun allowing curious citizens, and not just the bereaved, to board from the same City Island dock from which caskets and inmates embark. But on the raw morning in March when I was supposed to go, I got an email from the DOC advising that all visits to Hart were canceled. This wasn't, by then, a surprise. The next day, the governor would order all New Yorkers to put their lives on pause. Two weeks after that, images of Hart captured by a drone and published by Melinda Hunt would shock America. What the pictures showed—piles of plain pine coffins being covered with dirt—was no departure from the usual practice on this island for the past century, though few usually pay attention. All that was different was the number of coffins, and the fact that the workers in hazmat suits were not now inmates from a coronavirus-ravaged Rikers, but hands hired for the pandemic.

. . .

NOW HART'S FATE, WITH the city's budget underwater, looks unclear. But the larger arc of history its
name contains—from indigenous hunting ground to
colonial backwater to destination for the city's human
refuse to future nature refuge, perhaps, run by its Parks
Department—is shared by many of the small islands
here, which have perhaps begun, with the recent expansion of the city's ferry network, to again intrude on New
Yorkers' consciousness. And while there's no ferry yet that
will get you to Shooters Island, or even within sight of it,
it was by riding another of the city's new public boats, to
an event on a barge in Red Hook, that I finally got there.

The barge in question, an eighty-foot "covered deck-
house," once used to convey furniture and flour and
sewing machines to trains in New Jersey, wasn't the con-
veyance that would take me. The Lehigh Valley Railroad
Barge No. 79 has been moored to the Red Hook waterfront since 1994, by a man who bought it for $500 when
the vessel was filled with mud back in the eighties and left
for dead beneath the George Washington Bridge. David
Sharps cleaned No. 79 up and turned her into his home
before floating her to Red Hook and opening onboard a
humble museum to the "Lighterage Era," when barges
like this one bobbed by the hundred over the Hudson,
used for cargo transfer ("lighterage") before container

ships took over. On this day it was hosting a celebration, put on by the urban history organization City Lore, of "waterfront heroes," including the event's host; a veteran Sandy Hook pilot who'd spent his career meeting ships at the base of the Ambrose Channel, twelve miles out at sea, to guide them home; and a Sri Lankan nurse from Staten Island who, as a master of her homeland's distinctive song form known as kavi, performed a dirge in her native tongue about "the tale of Sandy's thunder."

As a pair of silver-haired men with banjos sang sea chanteys, I joined the day's honorees to inspect a hand-drawn map, used by Sandy Hook pilots, whose most notable feature was a spot by the Ambrose Channel labeled "Local Magnetic Disturbance." ("There's a whole lot of iron or something down there," said the Sandy Hook pilot. "Makes compasses go loopy.") I looked at a newspaper article from 1953 about a tugboat cook's recipe for Swedish meatballs. And I spoke to a nice man I know from the Historic Districts Council who, when he's not busy helping to save old buildings, is given to circulating invitations to readings of Walt Whitman's poetry convened on canoes in the Gowanus Canal. He told me that if anyone knew how best to visit Shooters under human power—my sporadic efforts to find a guide with the right boat or advice had to that point been frustrated—it was another waterfront hero who wasn't feted that day on the barge, but could have been.

Which is why and how one day months later I at last nudged out into the Kill Van Kull with Rob Buchanan. A boatbuilder and educator, Buchanan is a driving force behind the Billion Oyster Project. The organization, devoted to one day seeing its namesake bivalve again become the keystone species of New York, has in recent years helped students from the Harbor School on Governors Island, and across the city, seed more than a dozen new oyster reefs now helping to filter its waters. Buchanan is also known for crafting beautiful Whitehall rowboats (they're named after the base of Manhattan's Whitehall Street, where they were long made). On this day, though, we were floating in an outboard skiff he usually used to see oysters but which we'd today boarded by the Brooklyn Navy Yard to steer across the Harbor and, puttering up the Arthur Kill behind the huge Amazon fulfillment center on Staten Island's western shore, to skim past the Isle of Meadows (its name's still apt) and Prall's Island (named for a Dutch farmer who owned it): a bird refuge whose reedy edges teemed with crabs but whose avian population, Buchanan said, had in recent years declined thanks to the Parks Department's efforts to eliminate an invasive tree that was also its egrets' homes. As we emerged onto the Kill Van Kull, a towering freighter with HANJIN on its hull, no doubt guided by a Sandy Hook pilot, eased under the Bayonne Bridge. Hugging close to shore, Buchanan motored toward one of Shooters' decrepit piers. Many of the island's herons, Buchanan said, had for unknown reasons recently moved over to Hoffman. But one of the birds, wading in Shooters' shallows by a rotted hull, fixed us with a steady stare, or seemed to. And then, spreading its wings as we jumped out of the skiff to explore its home, it glided off toward New Jersey.

6.

BROKERS AND POWERS
(AND NEIGHBORHOODS, TOO)

If one were to narrate the basic stages by which the names that make up a city multiply and change, in step with its growth from hamlet to town to metropolis, one could identify—in a manner more schematic than how any city actually grows, but that's helpful nonetheless—some steps of evolution.

The first commences when a human settlement is formed, perhaps beside a river or bestride its mouth by the sea, and is named for its setting or its founders' sponsors. At this stage, the town—perhaps built around a fort, likely enclosed in a wall—gives to its clay or cobbled streets names that describe their role ("front," "bridge," "church," "wall"). Next come streets named for their denizens' vocations ("baker," "butcher," "abattoir"), or their uses ("water," "pearl," "bowling green"). Third come names, if the town thrives, that commemorate its worthies or hail its history, even as outlying areas—the farms beyond the old walls, and the lanes laid to reach them—

are named for their owners. Finally, and fatefully for the town that would become a city, arrives a shift signaled by a word that's nowadays used as often to describe a certain kind of place as it is a process.

"Subdivision": the term in modern usage calls to mind suburban tract homes and cul-de-sacs, but it's also the best word we've got to describe what began to happen, in the late 1700s, to the old farms of New York's first families. When the Stuyvesants and Delanceys and Bayards decided their large holdings were worth less under wheat than chopped up into blocks to be built up or sold off, they were at once responding to and shaping the expansion of a growing city. Not all of those families' initial schemes for subdivision worked out (and the Delanceys, though they've still got their namesake thoroughfare on the Lower East Side, had the job finished for them after they backed the British during the Revolution and were run out of town). But these first forays into large-scale subdivision transformed what was once New York's "Out Ward" into urban space—and augured two dynamics essential to how the city's neighborhoods, and the means by which we know and navigate them, have multiplied in space and time.

The first and simpler of these dynamics is hinted at by some of the more intriguing street names, both bygone and extant, in lower Manhattan. Before Elizabeth and Hester were addresses suggestive first of immigrant and now of hipster life on the Lower East Side, they were two cherished daughters of the Bayard clan whose old farm's grid, laid out in 1788, also included blocks called Art, Amity, and Science (now renamed). The diagonal course of Stuyvesant Street, in the East Village, suggests why you've likely never heard of the other roads of the Stuyvesant Farm Grid: Its angle differed from that of the Manhattan master plan later laid over it. (Among them were streets named for the Stuyvesants' own daughters—Judith, Eliza, Margaret—and others named for cities in the low corner of Europe—Rotterdam, Antwerp, Bruges—from whence their forebears came.) But to explore the city and its maps now is still to encounter similar odd clusters of street names. And from that curious portion of the Bronx whose avenues are named Caesar, Cicero, Cincinnatus, and Virgil to the bit of Brooklyn whose street names in sequence (Buffalo, Utica, Schenectady, Troy) don't just punctuate a walk through Crown Heights but evoke an eastward journey across upstate New York, the answer as to where they've come from, generally speaking, is clear. They're the fruit of subdivision: of a private developer or public commissioner having the chance to lend a mnemonic theme to some newly divvied-up pasture or freshly surveyed blocks. (Those upstate-themed streets in Crown Heights date from when new blocks were carved from Brooklyn's old Lefferts Farm by surveyors evidently eager, in the 1850s, to evoke a waterborne journey down the Erie Canal. The Roman streets in the Bronx were put there, in the 1920s, by a developer, Solon L. Frank, whose given name, shared with an Athenian sage, may or may not have fed his love for classics.)

That's the first import, for the student of names in the city, of subdividing its nether lands. The rendering of undifferentiated space into discrete places always occasions new names, many of them more inventive than the older ones. But there's a linked and larger reason that subdividing the "Out Ward" beyond its walls changes what the city is, and where it's heading. For this is the means and moment by which the city's very soil and bedrock, and the air above both, is turned into an urban commodity whose "use value," as the Marxists might say, is continually and ever more quickly outstripped by its price as a salable fiction—a number on a piece of paper or in the market's mind—to speculators. This is the signal moment in a defining activity of a city long animated by what Alexander Hamilton called its investors' "rage of getting rich in a day." Theirs is a particular faith, when it comes to real estate, long intrinsic to city life: that the price of its real estate will, day by day and year on year, charge ever upward like the "supertalls" that now line Central Park South and whose $100 million apartments in the sky aren't mainly places to live but to park and grow cash. And the truth that this faith has, year on year and decade by decade, by and large been borne out (with, of course, some notable exceptions when everyone took a bath) is a fact vital to how the city has grown up, how it's grown out, and who runs its show. John Jacob Astor may have made his first fortune with beaver pelts, but his heirs became New York's oligarchs thanks to his foresight in buying up big swaths of land ahead of where the city, which was growing fast in the early nineteenth century, wanted to go.

In those same years, the Manhattan financiers who invented what we call "investment banking" helped its governor dig a "big ditch" across the state whose opening in 1821 was hailed by those streets in Crown Heights. The Erie Canal's opening ensured that the East Coast's biggest city, now joined by water to the astonishing resources and raw materials of a vast hinterland, would become what Oliver Wendell Holmes termed "the tongue that is lapping up the cream of commerce and finance of a continent." North America's foremost port had declared its independence from Britain in the same year that James Watt, back in the old country to which New York's merchants stayed linked, perfected the steam engine that launched an industrial revolution. The city stepped onto its path toward becoming a global center of industry and finance just as the new economic engine that made Watt's revolution go—capitalism—whirred into high gear. These happenstances of history and of timing, to say nothing of the geography New York both inherited (its sublime natural harbor) and made (the canal to its west), were all vital to the story of how and why it became, within scarcely three centuries of its founding, the most populous and powerful and richest city on earth. But they don't in and of themselves tell you much about the particular shape New York took, or how its map grew. The terrific pace at which this happened saw even the pastoral northern reaches of the Bronx, by the early twentieth century, given over to new subdivisions, like one whose streets' names—Ampere, Ohm, and Watt—toast the wonders of electricity. (These were named in honor of Isaac Leopold Rice, an industrialist whose companies included, respectively, the Electric Storage Battery Company, Electric Boat Company, and Electric Vehicle Company, and who gifted his estate by Pelham Bay to the city after World War I.)

Capitalism has a tendency, observed Karl Marx, toward what he called "overaccumulation": that is, the creation of excess wealth, whether from investments in electric boats or in Pennsylvania pig iron, that it behooves the capitalist to plow back into the physical world—into building a bigger factory, a new railroad, a new housing complex for workers—to make still more of it. This is what the geographer and CUNY professor David Harvey has called the "spatial fix": the inbuilt effect and aim of capital not merely to regiment time but to alter space—to create ever more and better ways, in the world around it, to reproduce itself. At one time this took the shape, in New York, of ever more factories and warehouses; now luxury condos are its moneymaker. But the "spatial fix" isn't solely about private lucre. It can also be expended, in a functioning democracy wherein private excess is collected as tax, on public goods, such as schools that train

workers but also mold better citizens; roads that ease sup-
ply chains but also help people visit their grandmothers;
parks that raise nearby real estate prices but also make
the city more pleasant for everyone. And long before the
phrase "public-private partnership" became a cute euphe-
mism for developers fleecing City Hall, private interest
and public capital were being placed in sync by Robert
Moses, the notorious power broker who, for a vital span
of the twentieth century, controlled the city's planning
agenda, and thus much of the public purse, to a stunning
degree. Moses built more things that New Yorkers love—
bridges and beaches and playgrounds—than his nasty
reputation today may suggest. But both his casual racism
and his preference for cars over neighborhoods where
people without them lived were realized in infamous
projects like the Cross Bronx Expressway—a highway
he rammed across several communities of color, permanently scarring their borough (and the East Tremont area
most of all) in the 1950s. But such are some of the ways
that New York's neighborhoods, those essential building
blocks of city life from which residents forge vital sensi-
bilities of community and self, are made and unmade in
time.

THE FIRST NEW YORK CITY neighborhood to be widely
celebrated as such—as a discrete zone of the city, predicated on face-to-face interaction among residents, and

shaped by some sense of shared geography and mores—is an area now referred to, aptly enough, as the Village. This once-rural hamlet, a couple miles north of New York's colonial port, was dubbed Groenwijck ("green district") by a Dutchman who settled there before its name was Anglicized to Greenwich and it was incorporated into New York as an area—Greenwich Village—whose age and location south of modern Manhattan's grid let it retain its crooked streets. It was those streets' character that inspired Jane Jacobs, a Village resident who became a famed urban theorist, to describe certain of her neighborhood's virtues—its buildings' human scale; its mix of mom-and-pop businesses peddling wares its residents can afford; its "eyes on the street" whose owners' names one may not know but whose daily presence as nodding acquaintances any thriving neighborhood needs—in ways that have seen her canonized as the patron saint, and chief defender, of the city's neighborhoods against big-time developers and "big plans." This latter reputation was earned, beyond the success of her 1961 book *The Death and Life of Great American Cities,* by a campaign she led against Robert Moses's plan to ram one of his beloved highways straight down Fifth Avenue and across a park with a famous archway at the Village's heart.

That this protest prevailed is a fact for which generations of NYU students, and the weed dealers and buskers around the arch in Washington Square, can be grateful. But Jacobs's own legacy, as a "defender" of neighborhoods against the encroachments of capital, also isn't simple: Without her efforts at preserving the human-scale charm once known for its bohemians and bookstores, it is hard to picture the West Village's current phase as a luxury brand name with historic housing stock affordable only to the very rich. By the same token, the history of neighborhood-making in Manhattan of course didn't end when its Commissioners' Plan of 1811 laid out a new grid of streets, 220 blocks long, clear to Inwood's tip. The grid to come may have preordained the direction of New York's development, and the names (or, rather, numbers) of many of its future streets. But this didn't stop real estate mavens and residents, too, from coining novel names for Cartesian blocks of streets, meant to sell them or—in more plebeian districts—to distinguish them from others.

Not a few of the latter breed of name, in the city's scrappy *Gangs of New York*–era youth, seemed coined less to attract visitors than to repel rival gangs or attract curious sinners. The name of the red-light district in Midtown that was called Satan's Circus (not to be confused with Corlear's Hook, by the East River, from whose working women we likely got the term "hooker") didn't last. But that of nearby Hell's Kitchen did. Later on and higher up, neighborhood names meant to attract the well-heeled—Carnegie Hill, Lincoln Square, Lenox Hill—were attached to zones built up in their image. Where many of those labels have faded from daily use, a new sort of neighborhood name became common in the late twentieth century. Built by combining syllables from nearby landmarks or older districts into new words, these labels have proved extra-appealing to real estate agents and others for whom the term "neighborhood" connotes not neighbors but an agglomeration of amenities or prestige or cash.

The first one of these, SoHo, was in fact coined by an urban planner in 1962. But no marketer could have bested this succinct and jazzy abbreviation for the zone South of Houston Street, which also carried a tasty whiff, as the area's raison d'être moved from industry to arts, of the older Soho in London. There's a similar story behind TriBeCa (for Triangle Below Canal Street), whose name was coined by some artists in 1973 to describe a small tri-corner of blocks that is, in fact, right below Canal, but which is now applied, by hawkers of luxury lofts, to a far larger area that's not a triangle at all. NoLIta (North of Little Italy) and NoMad (North of Madison Park) were both coined by real estate people, more recently, to flog their sky-high rents. They haven't yet succeeded, though it's not for lack of trying, in rebranding a stubbornly poor piece of the Bronx which you'd think would be easier to gentrify, given its location just across the East River from Harlem. But having tried to help the South Bronx by calling it the "Piano District," they're now going with the awful appellation, SoBro, that one prays won't stick.

Such are the challenges inherent to dressing an older neighborhood in new clothes—and a new name—to sell it. No such hurdles existed for the namers of developments plopped onto former farms in the counties that in 1898 became, in the eyes of Manhattanites at least, the "outer boroughs." As these fields were bought and divvied up among developers of varied outlook and aim, some of the new communities they built seemed to embrace the influential Scottish city planner Patrick Geddes's loathing for "the gridiron plan"—a mode for organizing urban space with roots in the Roman camp whose simplicity and scalability commended it but whose fatal flaw, in Geddes's view, was its incapacity for addressing particulars of locale and site he called "topographic facts."

GEDDES'S FOREMOST AMERICAN ADMIRER was Lewis Mumford, the noted polymath and urbanist and son of Queens whose dozens of books ranged from *Technics and Civilization* and *The Transformations of Man* to *The Brown Decades: A Study of the Arts in America, 1865–1895.* Decades before Mumford published his most read book, *The City in History,* in the same year that Jane Jacobs published hers, he also served as a kind of in-house spokesman and scholar for the Regional Planning Association of America. This was a society of leading urbanists and planners founded in 1923 by the architect Clarence Stein and devoted to better synthesizing, for Americans of all income levels and in an ethical and humanist direction, the benefits of urban life with the virtues of nature.

Among the RPAA's bright ideas was the creation of the Appalachian Trail. In New York, its foremost success was also America's foremost expression of what germinated across the sea in Britain as the Garden City Movement.

The larger area of northwest Queens where this development was built has a name—Sunnyside—that sounds like a marketing tag plopped here by a modern developer to evoke banal warmth. In fact, it dates to 1713, when a Huguenot family called the Bragaws named their estate here Sunnyside Hill. But Sunnyside Gardens, designed by Clarence Stein and built here in 1924, was composed of sixteen blocks of varied but conjoined low-rise houses (including Lewis Mumford's home of many years) made from Hudson brick and grouped around communal gardens. Beyond its success as design and as place—Sunnyside Gardens is now listed on the National Register of Historic Places, and remains one of the city's stablest and prettiest middle-class neighborhoods—this planned community was also notable for conjoining evolved design and a social conscience with the world of big-time city real estate. The project's main financier, Alexander Bing, was a leading developer whose other projects included not a few of Manhattan's more august prewar apartment houses. Bing, playing against type, wasn't a philistine allergic to conceiving of public rather than private good: He was a good friend of Lewis Mumford's who delighted in proving to his developer friends, as he and his partners did with Sunnyside Gardens, that you could build well-designed housing for working people, on a tract whose buildings took up just twenty-eight percent of the land, as they did in Sunnyside Gardens, and still make six percent on your investment. But his was and is a business whose basic goal is to fill up any lot or building or bit of air rights with as much lucrative square footage, or rentable space, as possible. Most developers aren't as evolved as Bing. And Queens was filling up fast, in those years, with other subdivisions and planned communities built by developers following or anticipating wherever the subway reached next.

Until 1909, the area now called Jackson Heights was a mix of wetland and meadow called Train Marsh. But then a group of investors formed the Queensboro Corporation to buy three hundred acres here ahead of the arrival of what was called the IRT's Flushing line when it opened, but which straphangers now call the 7 train. The company's marketers named their development for the nearby thoroughfare then known as Jackson Avenue but called Northern Boulevard today, and added the "heights" in a bid to lend its blocks of six-story apartment houses, notwithstanding their low elevation, a bit of social prestige. (The corporation also pursued that end by banning from their new development, with the help of restrictive covenants, Catholics and Jews and residents of color.)

Nearby Elmhurst has older roots: It began as a Dutch village in the seventeenth century and was known until the late nineteenth by the name—Newtown—bequeathed it by the English. It got its current name thanks to a local booster and real estate man named Cord Meyer, who in 1897 convinced the town's elders that dissociating their community from smelly Newtown Creek, and renaming it for its elm trees, would be savvy. Meyer would go on to buy a passel of farms to Elmhurst's southeast, a few years later, whose fields he carved into a community, soon to be home to Tudor-revival homes and a famous tennis center, that he dubbed Forest Hills. Adjacent Kew Gardens, known for its own Anglophilic architecture (and, later on, for the murder of Kitty Genovese), was named by its developer for a botanical garden in London.

The truth that Corona, Queens, has in recent years become a Mexican enclave is a cosmic riddle of a piece with the fact that Jamaica is now home to many Jamaicans. But long before that happened, this onetime no-man's-land variously known as West Newtown or East Flushing got a new name from developers who wanted to tout "the crown of Queens."

One of those developers, an evidently inventive soul named Benjamin Hitchcock, was also behind the christening of another area developed in those years, down near Aqueduct Racetrack and alongside a new train line between Long Island City and Howard Beach. Today Ozone Park's name resonates as a home to many new immigrants from Trinidad and Guyana, whose Indo-Caribbean cuisine—including its trademark curried-chickpea-and-pepper sandwich called "doubles"—gets my vote for world's best street food. But when Hitchcock and company named it in 1882, they weren't thinking of either curry or global warming: Their concept, a century before we all learned the phrase "ozone layer," was to draw residents to the area by evoking the oxygen brought here by breezes off the Atlantic.

Sometimes, developments that never got built still left a mark. In 1905, the would-be makers of a subdivision near Jamaica where Jews would be welcome, and that they planned to call Utopia, ran out of money and the result—as suggested by the meaning of "utopia's" Greek roots, from "ou" (not) and "topos" (place) was "no place"—but not before building a road, which is still called Utopia Parkway, to its site. And sometimes, builders simply named developments after themselves. Today the name "Rego Park" puts one in mind of Bukharan bakeries and Russian Jews on Queens Boulevard. But its name was coined in 1925, whether as a lark or because they thought it good advertising, by the owners of the Real Good Construction Company that made it.

OVER IN STATEN ISLAND, such development schemes were rarer—at least until the building of the Verrazzano-Narrows Bridge. The city's least populous borough remains its most densely packed with both intriguing colonial names, invoking princes and mariners, and old-fashioned descriptive ones, too. For instance, Sandy Ground is where a coterie of Black homeowners bought property in 1829, after the end of slavery in New York, to found America's first "freedmen's village" by the South Shore's oyster beds. There are also towns named for stops on Staten Island's railroad (Pleasant Plains) and for soap (Port Ivory, home for many years to a very clean factory). The island's most notable prewar subdivision was built by its most prominent citizen. Cornelius Kolff, a real estate magnate who also wrote books including *The History of Staten Island* and a collection of local folklore called *Staten Island Fairies,* gave to his new tract of high-end homes overlooking the Narrows a name that was soon applied to its surrounding area, too: Shore Acres. When three decades later the Verrazzano's opening brought what felt like half the Italians in Brooklyn over the bridge with thoughts of staying, it's no accident that one of the developments built to house them in 1964—Heartland Acres—both riffed on Kolff's earlier project and seemed to promise immigrant ethnics aiming to finally "become American" that they could do so by making it as far west, anyway, as the heartland of Staten Island. (Some of Heartland Acres' streets were also named for astronauts from the Mercury, Gemini, and Apollo space programs of that decade.)

In Brooklyn, the history of developers coining names for new neighborhoods, or of "rebranding" old ones to attract a certain kind of resident, has deep roots. One example from the early years of the republic occurred near a stretch of the Brooklyn waterfront, aptly enough, that's grown synonymous with development companies run amok. Two hundred years before one such company, Two Trees, set out to rebrand some forlorn warehouses under the Manhattan Bridge as DUMBO (read: Down Under the Manhattan Bridge Overpass), Vinegar Hill was named by a man who hoped to attract, with a name honoring a fierce battle in the Irish Rebellion of 1798, Irish tenants (never mind that "vinegar" was a flawed English translation of a typically lyrical Gaelic place-name that would be more accurately rendered "hill of the wood of the berries").

Both Brooklyn and the Bronx, in general, followed different trajectories from Queens when it came to their neighborhoods' making. Much of Brooklyn's future map was set out by its Commissioners' Plan in 1839. By 1875, the western half of the Bronx had been annexed to New York (and incorporated into its grid). But where many old colonial and landowners' names in the Bronx, as a result, were retained by areas now turned industrial and urban, new neighborhood names did fill Brooklyn's map. Some of these were new developments—Bensonhurst-by-the-Sea, Dyker Heights—built up by the edges of old towns like New Utrecht. Others were names arrived at, by something like consensus, by homeowners and -builders of new districts built up after the Civil War to abut Prospect Park. In 1889, the *Brooklyn Eagle* ran a piquant letter from a group of readers arguing that among the several names then being used for the area we now call Park Slope—Prospect Hill, Park Hill Side, Prospect Heights (soon grabbed by another area abutting the park)—the name that eventually won out ("Slope is inappropriate, as it applies more to the side of a mountain, like the western slope of the Sierra Nevadas") was the worst.

Other neighborhood names here were new monikers for already built-up areas of what from the middle of the nineteenth century to the middle of the twentieth appeared on maps as undifferentiated parts of "South Brooklyn." Some of those names, like Sunset Park, sound like generic suburbia. Others, coined by community organizers or real estate agents or both, sound old but aren't. The name of Boerum Hill, for example, doesn't date from when its quite un-hilly acreage was a farm owned by a Dutch family called the Boerums. It was only affixed to their erstwhile land when a woman named Helen Buckler in 1964 founded the Boerum Hill Association to convince the city to turn her neighborhood's historic row houses into official city landmarks. At the time, it was a working-class area notable for a sizable enclave of Mohawk Indians—steelworkers, unafraid of heights, who helped build many of the city's skyscrapers and whose own name for their neighborhood here, Little Caughnawaga, invoked their homeland in Quebec. Once Boerum Hill was indeed made a historic district, many of its old inhabitants moved out, as seems often to be the case, in favor of new ones with much more money. Many of its affluent home buyers, today, have landed here after narrowing their search for the perfect slice of the mythic land known as "Brownstone Brooklyn" to this area and an adjacent one, whose own hilly label evoking the past—Cobble Hill—dates not from the nineteenth century, but from 1959. That's when devotees of its uncobbled blocks dusted off an old nickname for their home, not in use since the era of Andrew Jackson, and made it new. The less said about the new collective acronym by which the respective hills, Boerum and Cobble, and adjacent Carroll Gardens are now known to real estate agents—BoCoCa—the better.

It's a basic trait of the new gentrification to be predicated on some explicit whiff of Old New York—in housing stock or place-name or preferably both. But the look of the past, like that of the future, changes with time. And of course not all modes of place-making in New York, over recent decades, have involved the varied processes we now associate with that nebulous word, "gentrification"—coined by a British sociologist in the 1960s—that entered New York's parlance in the 1980s. Nor is the history of neighborhood-making in the city, in the twentieth century, only about citizens and sellers coining new names and identities for old zones or new subdivisions. For a key stretch of years after the Great Depression, the city's government and its allies in business and in Washington sought to build from on high, for better or for worse, new forms of urban habitation—and new kinds of neighborhoods—for the masses.

"DOWN WITH ROTTEN ANTIQUATED rat holes!" proclaimed Fiorello La Guardia in 1936. "Down with hovels, down with disease, down with firetraps. Let in the sun, let in the sky." The mayor had presided two years earlier over the founding of the United States' first public agency devoted to furnishing low-cost housing for its citizens. Now he was hailing the opening, on the Lower East Side, of the New York City Housing Authority's first project. Built on land bought from Vincent Astor and pointedly sited in a part of Manhattan known for its "lung blocks," where tuberculosis was epidemic, these New Houses, as they were called, would soon be joined by the Harlem River Houses in upper Manhattan (reserved for Black families) and the Williamsburg Houses in Brooklyn (reserved for white ones). Over the next thirty years NYCHA and its partners would build, sometimes with federal help but often without it, an archipelago of now-dilapidating projects whose 2,600 buildings, spread over 334 discrete developments, contain nearly 180,000 apartments and are home today to some 500,000 people.

Much of what's now said and written about NYCHA's city within a city focuses on its outposts' current sorry state. Conceived as springboards for working families to join the middle class, its projects' buildings have devolved with decades of disinvestment and deferred maintenance into holding pens for its most marginal. NYCHA, today, is in trouble. But its brick towers, invariably called "homes" or "houses" and rising singly or in groups from sprawling park-sized lots, have shaped the city's modern culture and politics in innumerable ways. And tracing their names' sources and shifting meanings suggests much about how and why.

When in the 1930s and '40s the first of these enticing places attracted piles of applications from New Yorkers eager to flee its rotting tenements, or who'd just returned from the war and were keen to raise kids in buildings boasting every modern convenience and green space outside, the documents required to move in—testaments to good character, work history, and even sufficient furniture—ensured that they were places intended for, and inhabited by, upstanding citizens of all backgrounds. Their names, in the era of "slum clearance," rarely recalled what they replaced (with the exception of beloved ballparks: There was no way the NYCHA project built atop the baseball Giants' erstwhile home, after Willie Mays and company left for San Francisco, wasn't going to be named the Polo Grounds Towers). They tended to use place-names already extant (Bronxdale, Baychester), or to describe their locus in other ways (Parkside), or to honor governors or presidents from the near or distant past

(Alfred E. Smith, Ulysses S. Grant). But then the populace and de facto purpose of NYCHA's housing projects changed, and with it their names' complexion.

New federal laws, stipulating that publicly funded housing be open only for the poor, not persons of mixed income, went into effect just as new forms of affordable housing in the suburbs and elsewhere—much more open to white home buyers than Black ones—saw the class and color composition of NYCHA's tenants radically change. Black majorities in its projects became pronounced in the same era that a national movement for civil rights saw a generation of city politicians avow its aims: NYCHA's naming habits, especially in Black neighborhoods, began to preview the city's later push toward street names and other place-names that honor its ethnic histories. Projects were named for heavyweight writers of the Harlem Renaissance—James Weldon Johnson, Langston Hughes—and for its era's back-to-Africa apostle, Marcus Garvey. Jackie Robinson got his inevitable project, and so did Dr. King. Less well-recalled servants of struggle also did: Bethune Gardens, in Washington Heights, is named for Mary McLeod Bethune, the founder of the National Council for Negro Women known during the Depression as "the Female Booker T. Washington." Some of these hat tips to Black freedom and pride, when encountered in the flesh, can sound patronizing. Whenever I walk past the NYCHA development nearest me in Manhattan, its signs welcoming residents and guests to the Frederick Douglass Houses, with their quote from the great man painted on rusting placards the city can't be bothered to fix, feel less than uplifting: IF THERE IS NO STRUGGLE, THERE IS NO PROGRESS.

The names of NYCHA projects that have grown known in the larger culture, during the decades that the system has been overwhelmingly peopled by New Yorkers of color, have more often been older ones lent new meaning by residents. When names like Farragut and Ingersoll and Marcy were stuck to NYCHA's first developments in Brooklyn, they honored a long-ago secretary of the Navy, an esteemed commissioner of parks, and—in the case of Mr. William Learned Marcy—a U.S. secretary of war whose execution of the Gadsden Purchase from Mexico, in 1854, won for the continental United States its final bit of territory. But now you can't say the word "Marcy" to any city dweller or music fan of a certain age without calling to mind the rapper and entrepreneur and bon viveur who put his home-place on their cognitive map. "I'm from where the hammers rung / news cameras never come," rapped Jay-Z on "Where I'm From," an early hit that saw him invoke a place where beef is inevitable but summertime's unforgettable, before summing up: "Marcy son / ain't nothing nice."

That the city's most suburban borough, Staten Island, also has a good deal of public housing would be a truth lost on many New Yorkers were it not for the rise to prominence of its own hip-hop heroes, the Wu-Tang Clan. The area of Staten Island called Stapleton was named for a Manhattan merchant, William Staples, who bought its land in 1836. But now "Staple-Land," as Wu-Tang member Ghostface Killah, described the Stapleton Houses where he grew up, "is where the ambulance don't come." When NYCHA's biggest development, the Queensbridge Houses, opened by the Queensboro Bridge in 1940, their twenty-six buildings housed lots of Irish and Italians and then GIs of all descriptions, happy to be home from the war. But after their white tenants left and those twenty-six buildings fell into disrepair and disrepute, the vibe changed. That this is a fact known to many people who've never been there is due to "Queensbridge" becoming a place-name that's also an idea and a leitmotif in the words and music of some of the city's finest modern poets. Where others of the biggest developments in the NYCHA system are known to few (no one beyond the Bronx speaks of Edenwald), they haven't produced hiphop greats like Nas, Mobb Deep, and the ones—Marley Marl and MC Shan—who in 1985 raised Bronx hackles by claiming that "The Bridge" was hip-hop's true home ("The monument is right in your face / Sit and listen for a while to the name of the place / . . . Queensbridge").

By the late 1960s and then into the '70s, the large presence of Puerto Ricans in neighborhoods where new NYCHA projects were built—the South Bronx, the Lower East Side, East Harlem—resulted in many of them being named for key figures in the island's long struggle, as a de facto colony of the United States, for dignity if not for freedom. When in 1950 the NYCHA complex that remains the largest in Manhattan was built in the part of the island that its Puerto Rican denizens call "Loisaida" (Lower East Side), it was named for the financier and statesman Bernard Baruch, who coined the term "Cold War" (and for whom CUNY's Baruch College is also named). Two decades later, things were different. To look up the names of the many NYCHA projects named for prominent Puerto Ricans in the seventies—from Ramón Betances (the leader of Puerto Rico's fight for independence from Spain in the nineteenth century), to Mariana Bracetti (the Boricua Betsy Ross who sewed the flag Betances's men flew), to Pedro Albizu Campos (who carried its ideals, and the fight for independence, not from Spain, but from the United States, into the twentieth)—is to gain a crash course in the modern saga of an island whose indigenous name, in 1980, became a part of NYCHA's map, too: It's there in Brooklyn's Borinquen Plaza. When a daughter of Borinquen who grew up in public housing in the Bronx was confirmed to the Supreme Court of the United States thirty years later, the project where she grew up—the Bronxdale Houses—was renamed for Sonia Sotomayor.

THE IMAGE OF THE city to come that most informed the architecture of much public housing, and which abets its failings now, was Le Corbusier's. Embraced by planners and builders from governments both communist and non- in the mid-twentieth century, his Ville Radieuse model was translated to the American context, and into English, as what Robert Moses termed "towers in the park." This model of housing, which looks as it sounds, sought to furnish, as Mayor La Guardia hoped, air and sun to the city's poor. But it failed to foresee that shunting them into generic towers without access to the things that make city life nourishing—vibrant street life and varied architecture, good schools and fresh food, decent jobs—was a recipe not for healthy neighborhoods, but for permanent marginalization (especially when projects were built, as often happened, in areas isolated from public transport or amenities). But NYCHA wasn't the sole builder of huge new developments that sought to conjure, with Robert Moses's help, a new kind of New York neighborhood after the vision of Le Corbusier.

At the 1939 World's Fair in Queens, the Metropolitan Life Insurance Company presented its vision of the urban future in the form of a massive scale model, complete with sixty thousand tiny windows, of a development its real estate arm was planning in the central Bronx. The name of MetLife's massive Parkchester complex, which opened three years later on the erstwhile grounds of a Catholic orphanage, was a portmanteau of the neighborhoods it sat between—Park Versailles and Westchester Heights—

and whose streets soon became known as "Parkchester,"
too. Its airy forest of dozens of mid-rise buildings, dotted with oval-shaped ponds and art deco flourishes, was
the model for another sprawling development built by
MetLife, this one in the East Village, whose 110 identical
red-brick buildings are just as hard to distinguish between
and thus to navigate, as anyone who's ever tried to find the
apartment of a friend there can attest. Stuyvesant Town–
Peter Cooper Village sits on land once owned by Peter
Stuyvesant, but which until the 1940s was occupied by the
building-sized gas-storage tanks and adjoining tenements
of the Gas House District that Robert Moses had razed,
during the war, on MetLife's behalf. For a half-century
after "Stuy Town" opened in 1947, it provided a rare oasis
of affordable housing for working families in a part of the
city that's become known for anything but. Affordable
rent, however, at least in New York always ends at some
point. When the Blackstone Group bought Stuy Town
a few years ago, they didn't spend $5.5 billion to charge
below-market rent.

More true to its original vision now is Co-op City in
the Bronx. Its thirty-five hulking towers occupy marshes
by the borough's end which until 1965 were home to the
Freedomland amusement park but now make up the
largest housing complex in the United States. Built with
help from a state program named for the legislators who
hatched it, MacNeil Mitchell and Alfred Lama, Co-op

City is also New York's largest "Mitchell-Lama," and a city unto itself distinguished by a particular form of ownership: To move in here, if one's lucky enough to get in off the waitlist, one buys an apartment by acquiring shares in the larger enterprise, whose cost is more akin to that of an economy car than a house. Monthly maintenance charges aid the upkeep of streets, here, that are named for an eclectic group of honorees—Pablo Casals, Amelia Earhart, Eugene Debs—whom the place's builders seem to have seen as the sort of paragons that Co-op City might also become, of human civilization in the twentieth century.

Today Co-op City may be more of a paragon, to some, of ongoing struggles to update its physical plant. But it's not in danger of succumbing to Stuy Town's fate: Its residents have remained firm in their determination, unlike members of other Mitchell-Lama co-ops who've voted to leave the program and sell their homes at market rates, to keep their towers by a swamp affordable until 2052. Also going nowhere is the other postwar development for New York dwellers of modest means that is big enough to appear on city maps. In Queens, near where Middle Village puts one in mind of Middle-earth (Middle Village is actually named for the midpoint on the road between the old towns of Williamsburg and Flushing), this development is called LeFrak City and it was built not by orcs but by the developer Samuel LeFrak, in 1971. LeFrak's eponymous thicket of seventeen-story apartment houses is still owned by his family company, the LeFrak Organization. The complex's name is an advertisement, both for its 15,000 tenants and for motorists rumbling by on the Long Island Expressway, for a big-time family in city real estate whose company, now led by Samuel's son Richard LeFrak, also built Manhattan's Battery Park City.

When in 1972 Samuel LeFrak's peer and rival Fred Trump bought a sizable stake in a LeFrak City–like development down by Jamaica Bay, he had thoughts of one day renaming Starrett City, as it's still called, Trump City instead. But where Fred was a magnate from the old school, content to sit back and collect rent, his son Donald—who grew up to become fast friends with Richard LeFrak—was made of more flamboyant stuff. It's not hard to imagine that when he set his sights on leveraging his outer-borough inheritance for the brighter lights of Manhattan, part of his inspiration for slapping the Trump name on any building he could was the LeFraks' landmark complex in Queens. The owners and makers of New York's built environment, the people who control what for two centuries has been its primary store of capital—its real estate—have long been the unseen kingmakers in its politics. The trick pulled off by Donald Trump, thanks less to his dealmaking than to his salesman's talent for self-promotional lies, was to leverage a career in buildings into one on TV that he then used, in the most improbable New York real estate story of all, to become his own kingmaker on a stage bigger even than Manhattan.

IN THE MANHATTAN THAT Trump left for the White House, the Midtown tower he built as a monument to his developer's id is no aberration. The rigged conflict between the people who own New York and the quaint notion we once called the "public interest" was settled long ago: It was won, with the help of the city's first billionaire mayor, Mike Bloomberg, by the developers. Even progressive-minded stewards of City Hall are now reduced to ordering the builders of ever-taller castles in the sky ("essential for the tax base," they say) to include a few affordable units, perhaps accessible by a "poor door" out back, for plebes. The Midtown blocks around Trump Tower were subject in 2017 to a controversial "upzoning" that recently saw Chase Bank, for example, buy the air rights over St. Patrick's Cathedral, for the purpose of blotting out the sun with a new seventy-story tower, several blocks distant. Elsewhere in the city, even the embattled chiefs of NYCHA, facing billions in debt and deferred maintenance, are getting in on this act: "Towers in the park" designs do at least contain, for the willing seller, beaucoup unexploited air rights. And in the meantime, every major addition to the city's physical plant in recent years—from Hudson Yards to Atlantic Yards to the Oculus and Chelsea Market—are anti-urban in spirit and effect: private spaces, built for private ends, that masquerade as public ones by allowing people to come buy frozen yogurt (but not to shape or inhabit the spaces in any meaningful way).

David Harvey, theorizer of the "spatial fix," has also written with trenchant force about what he calls the "right to the city"—the principle that every citizen of the city has a right not merely to be here, but to take part in its future's shaping. Jane Jacobs, in her enduring exegeses of how and why urban neighborhoods built at human scale "work" both for and with the help of those who live in them, wrote, "The cities and the economies we have, have been created by ordinary people who didn't have to have a big plan." That the fight against "big plans" was also a fight for neighborhoods in her day felt plain: The need to protect the Village's quirks from Robert Moses's bulldozers was urgent. The enemy, a half-century on, is more insidious. The West Village building where Jacobs lived over a candy shop, on Hudson Street by Perry, is now home to a real estate brokerage. But as she and our wiser city planners know, "big plans," and little ones, too, often don't turn out as planned. And the city's people, pulling meaning from the grid, have always had a way of making places—and of naming them—for themselves.

7.

HONORS AND SOUNDS

Among the hundreds of streets and corners that have in recent years been awarded honorary names in New York, it's a fair bet that only one of them was already the subject of a beloved song about how to reach it. In November 1969, the National Educational Television network, forerunner of PBS, first aired the signature theme of a soon-to-be-ubiquitous kids' TV show: "Can you tell me how to get, how to get to Sesame Street?" For fifty years, that query had no literal answer beyond the soundstage in Queens where *Sesame Street* is shot. But one fall evening in 2018, the CEO of Sesame Workshop, Jeffrey Dunn, revealed that this would change. He relayed the news to a crowd of smiling baby boomers, and one interloping writer, in a carpeted ballroom on West 65th Street.

"We tried to get the city to give us the stretch of Broadway out front," said Dunn, gesturing to the building that's long housed the nonprofit which was formerly known as the Children's Television Workshop. "They said, 'No, Broadway is Broadway. But 63rd between Broadway and the park—that's all yours.'"

The occasion was the launch of a new organization devoted to marking *Sesame Street*'s fiftieth birthday. The Sesame Workshop Alumni Network ("SWANs, if you like," said Dunn) had brought together a cheering roomful of puppeteers, writers, and actors with faces as familiar as Bert's and Ernie's. These included Sonia Manzano, known to millions of us who grew up watching her as Maria, and Emilio Delgado, whose character Luis, the kind-eyed proprietor of the Fix-It Shop, Maria joyously wed in 1988. "When I was growing up in the South Bronx," Manzano told me, "no one—no one—on TV looked like me. So when *Sesame* came on with Gordon and Susan, it was a huge deal." Manzano, the first Latina with a regular role in any program on U.S. national TV, had been drawn to join the show's cast in the early 1970s by its creators' determination to reach kids of all backgrounds by reflecting, in the show's makeup, the makeup of America. Now she and her fellow SWANs cheered Dunn's announcement. But they weren't the only people whose hearts would soon warm at glimpsing an actual New York street sign hailing an enterprise that was first launched to "take the addictive qualities of television and do something good with them."

With short, bright segments that mimicked the look of advertisements, the show enlisted an ingenious young puppeteer named Jim Henson to make those segments sing. The result, with the help of Cookie Monster and Grover and other of Henson's creations soon beloved by preschoolers everywhere, was a program that's won 189 Emmys and counting to become not merely the all-time champ of television for kids, but the most successful program of any kind in TV history. Which would all seem to be sufficient grounds for making *Sesame Street*'s name a permanent part of New York. And which also helps explain why, when on a raw spring morning a few months after Dunn's announcement I tromped down Broadway with my toddler for the unveiling of an actual New York City street sign labeled "Sesame Street," we found a much bigger crowd than usually turns out for such ceremonies when they're honoring local activists or beloved Little League coaches in the outer boroughs.

Kids joined grown-ups in Snuffleupagus sunglasses around a temporary metal stage upon which Sonia Manzano and Roscoe Orman, better known as Gordon, shared space with sundry Muppets and men in suits. The mayor, a politician of notable unpopularity and notable height, gave a speech. In it, he claimed to be Big Bird's long-lost cousin and praised what "Sesame Street" had meant to his own mixed-race family. Then he stepped from the stage to avail himself of a photo op with cherished public figures that no politician would turn down. The mayor joined his tall feathered kin, and grinned as Big Bird's big yellow hand reached upward to uncover a green street sign whose letters spelled out "Sesame Street." The crowd cheered. The local news crews got their shots. The commuters of Midtown, rushing past, barely skipped a beat.

There, amid Midtown's towers and across the avenue from Lincoln Center, the city's literal Sesame Street didn't look much like the pretend one with its homey brownstones and friendly neighbors sitting on stoops. But now this iconic site in our New York of the imagination has gained a literal site in its actual geography, joining the nearly 1,700 city byways and street corners that have, as of this writing, been bequeathed an honorary name by City Hall.

OF COURSE, EVERY STREET name in the city that hails a person's name or memory is, in a sense, "honorary." So are all those landmark bridges and tunnels and other bits of civic infrastructure that tend, whether named for a Kennedy or a Roosevelt or a Cuomo, to eulogize men more deft at pulling power's levers than Bill de Blasio is. But the more recent spate of honorary co-namings, of the sort that made Sesame Street real, date only from 1992. That's when New York's City Council passed Local Law 28. This is the statute allowing for streets and corners to be granted honorary "co-names" without having to change New York's official map—an onerous bureaucratic and legal hurdle whose removal from the process, along with a tacit understanding among City Council members that they'd ratify any co-naming proposed by their colleagues, has since resulted in a flood of new signs across the five boroughs.

Before 1992, the couple dozen new honorary names that were forced over the requisite hurdles by determined Council members and community boards celebrated revered pastors and rabbis, storied local pols, or police or soldiers killed in duty's line. Also, of course, ballplayers: A pair of beloved Yankees who died before their time (Lou Gehrig, felled by his namesake disease in 1941, and Thurman Munson, the mustachioed catcher who perished in a plane crash in 1979) got blocks named for them by Yankee Stadium. Also notable in the Bronx, among pre-1992 honorary name changes, is the city's only one of these to be added to the official map but later removed. This dubious distinction belongs to Dr. Theodore Kazimiroff, a dentist who once pulled a tooth from a live lion in the Bronx Zoo, but whose larger claim to fame, among devotees of the Bronx, was his serving as the city's first official historian. In 1981, a leafy stretch of Southern Boulevard by the zoo was officially named Dr. Theodore Kazimiroff Boulevard—before the city then decided, three decades later and in recognition that few local residents or businesses had taken to using addresses including the overlong phrase, to erase his moniker from its namesake blocks. Kazimiroff's widow, reached by the *New York Times* after this occurred in 2011 (the city, bowing to pressure, retained her husband's tag as an honorary co-name), remarked: "It's a slap in the face."

But New York's hubris-filled leaders have always seemed more willing than their peers in other American cities that are in love with their own pasts to countenance evolving its map. Far be it for, say, the worthies of New Orleans to ever entertain the notion of meddling with street names like Bourbon or Esplanade or Desire, so rich already in story and myth. Even lefty-loosey San Francisco has only seen fit to rechristen one of its major thoroughfares, in recent decades, for its modern values (that would be the erstwhile Army Street, in the city's historically Latino Mission District, which in 1995 became Cesar Chavez Street). New York's postwar craze for such gestures, by contrast, got under way when Mayor Fiorello La Guardia convinced the City Council, in 1945, to go along with his plan to rename Sixth Avenue the Avenue of the Americas. This doomed bid at boosting the profile of an unglamorous roadway was pitched by La Guardia as "an expression on the part of our people of the love and affection we have for our sister republics of Central and South America." But thus was born what would become a New York tradition: the foisting onto old streets of new names for which New Yorkers, as often as not, have no use.

After the Civil Rights movement, New York joined the 730 communities, across the land, that in the 1970s and '80s gained streets named for Martin Luther King Jr. In many of those places, such streets became colloquially known as "MLK," but New Yorkers have never used those initials to describe the main drag in Harlem that was officially dubbed Martin Luther King Jr. Boulevard in 1984: Its old name, 125th Street, was already indicative of Black freedom and pride, and more concise. But Harlem's civic leaders also went further, in those years, affixing the names of other Black luminaries to other street corners and avenues in the Black Mecca. These new names either lodged to some degree in local parlance (Frederick Douglass for Eighth Avenue, Adam Clayton Powell Jr. for Seventh Avenue) or didn't: Malcolm X was a Harlem icon who both built his following in the neighborhood and died there, but even his name can't compete with that of the famous thoroughfare—Lenox Avenue—to which it was stuck in 1987. This fact has nothing to do with local residents' reverence for the Gilded Age philanthropist and book lover for whom Sixth Avenue's northern reaches were named in 1887; it has everything to do with the decades' worth of lore and legends that accrued along blocks whose traffic Langston Hughes dubbed "Harlem's heartbeat," and in shouting distance of the late, lamented Lenox Lounge. The only people I know of, in any case, who call Lenox "Malcolm X" are affiliates of Harlem's Allah School in Mecca.

The year that Harlemites were surprised to see Malcolm's name appear on street signs there, the *New York Times* ran a story about how such name changes were out of control in the city. The article began with a business owner in the South Bronx who described looking out his window to find, one day, that a familiar street sign for Walnut Avenue had been replaced with one informing him that his block was now named Rose Feiss Boulevard (for the founder of a nearby manufactory of lampshades, though he'd never heard of her). Then the story explained how such shifts were much harder to push through in cities like Boston (where all property owners on a street had to be informed of name changes being considered) and San Francisco (where a majority of property owners don't merely have to be informed of a proposed change, but sign a petition requesting it). In New York, anyone willing to do the requisite politicking with their community board and Council member (including, say, family members of Rose Feiss in the Bronx) could push through a change without telling any property owners or local residents at all. This situation, and the confusion it had begun to cause, is a big part of what led to the passing of Local Law 28, in 1992: The City Council collectively decided to stop abusing its prerogative to permanently alter the city's map and instead just award honorary second names to mirror what ultimately happened with La Guardia's Avenue of the Americas (which, in 1984 and at the direction of Ed Koch, finally got back its "Sixth Avenue" street signs to go with its "Avenue of the Americas" ones).

The year that the new law went into effect coincided with the quincentennial of Columbus's arrival to the New World: Multiple city chapters of the Knights of Columbus succeeded in having their namesake honored

with street names like the one in Italian Bensonhurst—
Cristoforo Colombo Boulevard—that use his name's
Italian form. For the next few years, the pace of new
co-names held steady at a few dozen per. But then came
9/11. Council members availed themselves of the solemn
chance, in its attacks' wake, to honor their dead by affixing new co-names, belonging to first responders and
workers at the World Trade Center alike, to hundreds
of streets across the five boroughs. Perhaps this efflorescence of new names on New York's streets, which gave
the Council practice at adding them quickly, is what burst
the dam. In any case, the years since have witnessed an
ever-expanding list of new co-names that serve, for Council members, as a go-to means for making constituents
happy. By the late 2010s, the mayor was signing bills to
attach upward of 150 second names to its streets. And
the great majority of them are used less for navigation
than for photo ops like the one that countless devotees
of punk rock have availed themselves of in Manhattan's
East Village: the New York street sign—for Joey Ramone
Place—that's said to be stolen more often than any other.

This state of affairs, depending on your vantage, is
either a disaster of promiscuous place-naming or pretty
cool. Either way, the full list of honorary co-names rati-
fied since Local Law 28's passing comprises a second-
order geography laid atop the city's official map: a web
of iconicity which at least gestures toward the maps of
meaning that the inhabitants and makers of New York's

neighborhoods—or the local pols, anyway, who represent them in City Hall—are creating all the time.

THE CITY'S EVER-GROWING LIST of second and honorary names isn't now one that cabbies or mapmakers, thankfully, need to keep up with. This didn't stop the list's proliferating entries—whose rationales and backstories weren't publicly announced or recorded in an accessible way until 2014—from confounding curious New Yorkers. But then one such resident of the East Village, wondering why her block of East 4th Street was now also called Frieda Zames Way, wrote Manhattan's official borough historian, Mike Miscione, to ask if he had a comprehensive list of honorary street names and their sources. Miscione said he didn't. He called his friend Gilbert Tauber, a retired city planner and local history buff who had by then earned a reputation among his peers as, in Miscione's words, our "go-to streets guy." Tauber, fascinated by the evolution of street names in the city, had spent years researching the origins and stories of the hundreds that once graced its map but no longer do: If you ever find yourself needing to know where Oyster Pasty Lane ran (it's now Exchange Alley), or the antique name for what's now West 17th Street between Sixth and Seventh Avenues (that would be Paisley Place), Tauber's your guy, too. Now he accepted a new challenge. Consulting the appropriate sources, he compiled a master list of honorary street names added to the city's books since 1992, complete with capsule biographies for Frieda Zames (she was the president of Disabled in Action of New York) and an ever-growing list of 1,700 others. Thanks to Tauber's yeoman efforts, and a Web developer friend who helped him build an excellent website called Oldstreets .com (where you can also learn that Ms. Zames's namesake block on East 4th Street was once called Ragpickers Row), his annotated database of both bygone and honorary street names is now available for perusal by anyone with Internet access.

Not the least of the pleasures of perusing Tauber's list, for the name hound or pattern seeker enamored of meaning-making in the city's streets, are the trends and tendencies that emerge when going through its entries borough by borough, or all at once. A plurality of those signs, across the city, honor people—whether first responders killed at work or kids hit by cars—who died untimely deaths. But every borough has its distinctions. Manhattan, as you'd expect, has the most signs hailing celebrities. Staten Island, with its neighborhoods full of firemen and cops and people who rode the ferry to office jobs in the Twin Towers before 2001, has the most for victims of 9/11. If streets named for monsignors are your thing, then Queens (it's got five) is king. The Bronx has twenty-nine streets co-named for reverends, and two for tunes once crooned by its teens in the birthplace of doo-wop (they're hailed by a pair of street signs, in Morrisania, reading "The Chantels Hit Record 'Maybe' 1958" and "The Chords Hit Record 'Sh-Boom' 1954"). Every borough has streets named for detectives and for owners of pizzerias. But only Brooklyn boasts Harry Rosen Way–Cheesecake Corner, named for the man who opened what's been the borough's go-to spot for super-caloric desserts—Junior's—since 1929. Queens has no fewer than ten streets honoring men named Frank.

Among the choreographers and dancers who've now got streets, in this city on the move, are Jerome Robbins and Alvin Ailey and—though if you encountered O'Donnell Way you might think it honored a cop—May O'Donnell, an associate of Martha Graham and a titan of modern dance, whose name is on East 7th Street.

Alongside Manhattan streets named for actors ranging from well known (Katharine Hepburn), to less so (Jerry Orbach), to married (Ossie Davis and Ruby Dee, who've got his-and-hers signs on their old Harlem block) is one named for the famous Method acting teacher (Lee Strasberg Way, down in the Village). There's no shortage, from Sholem Aleichem to Zora Neale Hurston, of honored writers. More distinctive are streets named for their books, like Harlem's Manchild Way (it celebrates Claude Brown's novel *Manchild in the Promised Land*). No filmmakers, yet, have namesake streets. But the block where Spike Lee shot *Do the Right Thing,* in Brooklyn's Bed-Stuy in 1989, has since 2015 been called Do the Right Thing Way. In Jackson Heights, Queens, there's a street named

Manny "The Wrong Man" Balestrero Way: It honors a local man who was arrested for a robbery he didn't commit in 1953 and saw his ordeal turned into a film that Alfred Hitchcock shot in Balestrero's neighborhood.

Louis Liotta Way, in Brooklyn, recalls a noted photojournalist of sports and other pastimes who got his start tending the pigeons responsible, after Brooklyn Dodgers games at Ebbets Field, for flying film to the Acme Photo Agency in Manhattan. Not a few ballplayers who plied other trades at that cherished stadium before their team moved west are now commemorated, natch, on Brooklyn's streets. Jackie Robinson's smashing of baseball's color barrier, and his name, are recalled by both an expressway to Queens and a city block in Bed-Stuy. His teammate Carl Erskine, a pitcher whose nickname was "Oisk" among holders of old-school Brooklyn accents and who isn't too well known to people of other descriptions, is hallowed enough here to have given his name, in 2002, to the Erskine Interchange off the Belt Parkway. In nearby Midwood, the namesake block of the Dodgers' beloved first baseman Gil Hodges, who became the manager of the Mets and whose name's also on a bridge to the Rockaways, recalls an era when our sporting heroes didn't live in weird mansions in the suburbs, but among us. Less famous than Hodges but no less cheers-worthy was Betty "Moe" Trezza, who quit her job as a seamstress, during World War II, to become a standout utilitywoman in the All-American Girls Professional Baseball League, and who you can now find honored, in East Williamsburg, on Betty "Moe" Trazza Way.

If you were to mention to Brooklynites of a certain age that there's now a byway in the borough called Campanella, most would assume its named for the Dodgers' lionized catcher (and second Black player). But they'd be wrong. While there is a high school named Roy Campanella in Gravesend, Angelo "Chubby" Campanella Way in Bensonhurst honors a beloved ice-cream vendor, who during a decades-long career slinging frozen treats committed acts of heroism that included pulling a mother and child from a burning car, using his ice-cream truck to block a road to capture a hit-and-run driver, and "[donating] countless ice cream cones to children who were short of change." And Chubby is not the only purveyor of ice cream to be so honored. The South Bronx has Alfredo Thiebaud Way: It hails the creator of Delicioso Coco Helado, the coconut-flavored sweet that Thiebaud began concocting in his apartment in 1967 and sold in paper cups from a fleet of carts that's outlived him. Which means that, surprisingly, there are as many streets named for vendors of frozen treats as for legends of the sport that's become, in the decades since the Dodgers and the baseball Giants both fled west, the city's best-loved. Basketball is "the city game," so you might think that more of its players would be honored on New York's streets. But only two are. Dwayne "The Pearl" Washington Way, named for the streetball legend, is in Brownsville. Anthony Mason Way, which hails the cult-favorite Knicks forward from the 1990s who died before his time, names a piece of Rockaway Boulevard near where "Mase" grew up, in Ozone Park.

Would that Cyndi Lauper, another product of Ozone Park, might one day be honored with Girls Just Want to Have Fun Way. But in this city that's long seen itself as a mosaic of enclaves, its various ethnic and other communities have seen fit to herald their presence, or not, in their neighborhoods' streets, in contrasting ways. The Greek Americans of Astoria, Queens, seem to have taken particular pride in their impress on local media. The neighborhood doesn't merely boast blocks called AKTINA FM Way and Cosmos FM Way (they're named, respectively, for a pathbreaking Greek-language radio show that began airing on WNYE in 1993, and a station that began broadcasting Greek content around the clock a few years later). Astoria's got corners, too, named for the owner of National Greek Television (that would be Demetris Kastanas, aka "Mr. Greek TV") and also—though you'd need to read Greek to make out its lettering—for the *National Herald,* a venerable Greek-language daily founded in 1915 whose name in Anglicized Greek would sound like Ethnikos Kyrix Way.

In Dominican-dominated Washington Heights, local leaders have imported Santo Domingo's love for monuments to leave few corners in the neighborhood *un*adorned with signs hailing Dominican freedom fighters and sluggers and scribes—and succeeded, in 2000, in seeing St. Nicholas Avenue clear from 162nd Street to 193rd co-named for a founding father of the Dominican Republic, Juan Pablo Duarte. The Latin American custom of hailing history with calendar dates is also in evidence: 27 de Febrero Way commemorates the date that Duarte helped the DR win its independence, in 1844, from an army of occupying soldiers from the country— Haiti—with which it shares an island and whose émigré citizens in New York, across the city in Brooklyn, now also hail their own nation's founders in street-name form.

There in Flatbush, the stretch of Nostrand Avenue, now co-named Toussaint L'ouverture Boulevard, hails the figurehead of Haiti's revolution in the 1790s: He led a half-million enslaved Africans who fought to seize their freedom, for themselves, in what was then the French-owned sugar colony of Saint-Domingue. Nearby Jean-Jacques Dessalines Boulevard hails the general who succeeded L'ouverture in that struggle and pronounced the constitution, in 1804, of "a nation where . . . no white man will set foot as master." The street sign for the latter Haitian hero, when it was installed in 2018, drew protests from right-wing provocateurs who felt that Dessalines's history of violence—he was known for massacring his ex-colony's masters—made him an unworthy candidate for public praise in New York City (this notwithstanding the violent means by which the leaders of America's Revolutionary War, and countless other white war heroes honored on New York's streets, pursued their aims). Less controversial but also an icon of Haitian New York is another Toussaint who was, unlike Dessalines or L'ouverture, a New Yorker. Pierre Toussaint was born enslaved in the Caribbean, but came to New York with his owners in 1787 before buying his freedom with earnings from his work as a hairdresser. A devoted Catholic, he became known for his benevolence to the city's orphans and toward its sick during the yellow fever epidemic of 1803, after doctors fled the city. Pierre Toussaint is the only layperson now entombed among New York's cardinals in St. Patrick's Cathedral, and was named "venerable" by New York's Cardinal O'Connor in 1989, putting him on the path to sainthood. If you'd like to visit with his memory, you've been able since 2019 to do so at the corner of Church and Nostrand in Crown Heights.

Speaking of saints, Mother Cabrini, the unofficial *comare* of all Italian Americans, was the first American citizen to be officially named one by the Pope. Born Maria Francesca Cabrini in Lombardy, Italy, in 1850, she became known for her work on behalf of immigrants during the big wave of migration to New York from her homeland around the turn of the last century, and has for decades been an official part of New York's map: Cabrini Boulevard, in upper Manhattan, got its name in the year of her beatification, 1938. But her legion of admirers, perhaps aware that even many residents of that street don't know to whom its name (like that of Chicago's now-destroyed

Cabrini-Green housing projects) refers, have in recent years ensured that her full name also grace New York's streetscape in other ways: Today, stockbrokers can take their lunch in Mother Frances Xavier Cabrini Triangle, near where she began her work at St. Joachim's church in 1889. In 2017, on the centennial of her death, East 19th Street by Gramercy Park became Mother Cabrini Way. By then, another sainted mother had joined New York's streets. The name of Mother Teresa was affixed to a block off Pelham Parkway in the Bronx in 2009. Why there? Pelham Parkway is home to many Albanian Americans for whom the memory of their countrywoman, canonized for work with India's poor in 2016, is extra-dear.

This style of honorary name—the hailing of a prominent countrywoman or -man who's never been to New York—is also glimpsed elsewhere in the Bronx. Oscar de la Renta Boulevard doesn't mark a place that was significant to the august designer (who split his time, natch, between Connecticut and the Upper East Side), but it does hail a famous Dominican in a place where pride is fierce among the immigrant group that remains New York's most numerous—for now. Dominicans may soon be surpassed by another nationality—the Chinese—who now number more than eight hundred thousand in greater New York, and have established sprawling new enclaves around Flushing, Queens, and in southern Brooklyn. But for years, the sole honorary street name in any of New York's Chinatowns was in the original one, in Lower

Manhattan, that's still home to some hundred thousand mostly Cantonese-speaking Chinese. And it doesn't honor a community leader or modern immigrant: Commissioner Lin Ze Xu Square, off East Broadway, commemorates the officer appointed by his emperor, in 1838, to rid his people of the scourge of opium being pushed upon them by the British East India Company. His campaign to do so saw Lin Ze Xu launch and then lose a conflict recalled in England as the Opium War, but also win renown among his countrymen for the moral triumph of managing to destroy, before the war, 2.6 million pounds of narcotics. The commissioner's namesake square was joined, in 2013, by a nearby street named for a soldier of lower rank: Danny Chen Way was named for a private in the U.S. Army who committed suicide, while serving in Afghanistan, after being subjected to racist bullying by superior officers.

IN RECENT YEARS, the question of whose histories we commemorate on our cities' streets, and the heritage and gender of those honored, has become a topic of fierce debate. In New York, the truth that the city's map comprises what Rebecca Solnit calls a "manscape," as do those of most every city thus far made by humans, has fed new attention to the gender imbalance of its monuments. While New York has long had statues of imaginary women—Central Park's got Alice in Wonderland, the Harbor's got Ms. Liberty—the tally of statues honoring actual historical men versus those hailing women who in fact existed stood, until recently, at 145 to 5 (including the figure of Harriet Tubman dedicated in Harlem in 2008). In 2020, a long-gestating effort to start correcting this imbalance saw the unveiling, in Central Park, of a statue of the trailblazing suffragists Susan B. Anthony, Elizabeth Cady Stanton, and Sojourner Truth. But long before these developments and a mayoral initiative called She Built NYC, the push to see more women honored in the city's public spaces began not with statues but with streets. Years before Harlem got its Harriet Tubman statue, thirty blocks of St. Nicholas Boulevard there were co-named in her honor. And a decade before it was announced that a statue of Shirley Chisholm—the trailblazing Black congresswoman from Brooklyn who also became the first woman to seek the nomination of a major party for president—was going up by Prospect Park, a corner in Crown Heights was dubbed Shirley Chisholm Way.

Chisholm's friend and fellow federal legislator Bella Abzug got a street sign in 2017; it's in the Village, right near Jane Jacobs Way. And among the hundreds of other prominent and not-so-prominent women whose names have become streets since 1992 are tenant advocates and freedom fighters and poets—and one woman who was all of the above. Julia de Burgos Way, which follows East 106th Street clear from Fifth Avenue to the river, honors a famous poet who was also a fierce advocate for Puerto Rican freedom. Reproductive rights, if not the now-controversial racist views of the activist and educator who coined the term "birth control," are hailed in Margaret Sanger Square (it's next to Planned Parenthood New York's longtime headquarters, in the Village). Civil rights, and more radical modes of organizing for justice, are celebrated, too: Harlem's got streets named for Fannie Lou Hamer and Ella Baker. Mirabal Sisters Way, in Washington Heights, recalls the struggle of three brave "butterflies" martyred by the Dominican dictator Trujillo (and later celebrated in Julia Alvarez's novel *In the Time of the Butterflies*). The name of Sylvia Rivera, the campaigner for gay and transgender rights who threw the first bottle at Stonewall in 1969, has since 2004 graced the nearby corner of Christopher and Hudson. Bushwick won a street for the crusading Black journalist and anti-lynching advocate Ida B. Wells. In Brooklyn Heights, Emily Warren Roebling Way has since 2017 honored the woman who made building the Brooklyn Bridge possible, by replacing her husband as its chief engineer after he took ill, and she was duly honored as the first person to walk across it in 1887.

Another resonance for the number "87," and a sadder one, inheres in Ochenta y Siete (Eight-Seven) Boulevard in the Bronx. It's named for the dark night in 1990 when a disturbed man named Julio Gonzales, after a fight with his girlfriend, used a dollar's worth of gasoline to set fire to the Happy Land nightclub that claimed the lives of eighty-seven mostly Honduran immigrants. (Reverend Abner Bernard Duncan Way, nearby, recalls a preacher who was extra-helpful to victims' families in Happy Land's aftermath.) Other untimely deaths have been joined to already colorful lives. Joe "the Great" Rollino was a Coney Island strongman, all of five foot two inches tall, who once lifted 475 pounds with his teeth—and who died at 104, not of old age but from being struck, one morning while out for a walk on Bay Ridge Parkway, by a minivan. Other such untimely deaths, when befalling the young, have been joined to ennobling aims after they occur. Brooklyn's Briana Ojeda Way, in Boerum Hill, recalls an eleven-year-old girl who died after an asthma attack whose danger could have been dodged if a police officer flagged down by the girl's mother had been willing and able to perform CPR. Her parents' resultant crusade for the passage of "Briana's Law" finally saw the governor sign a statute, in 2019, requiring all New York safety officers to be trained in and ready to use CPR at all times. In Staten Island by Clove Lakes Park, a promising high school athlete who died from exposure to lethal amounts of methyl salicylate, the active ingredient in muscle rubs like Bengay, and whose passing "brought attention to the dangers of excessive use of such products," is recalled by Arielle Newman Run.

Bringing attention to poor Arielle Newman's home borough, New York's least heralded, hasn't often been easy. But among the few who've succeeded in doing so, none have matched the Wu-Tang Clan. The mighty hip-hop ensemble's nine core members all grew up in or around the borough's Park Hill neighborhood, but they developed their complex artistic identity—and their mythic geography of New York—by cutting class to ride the Staten Island Ferry to Manhattan and spending truant days in the old grindhouse theaters off Times Square. I once interviewed RZA, their leader, about how the kung fu flicks that he and his friends Raekwon and Ghostface Killah saw there, and growing up on an island they took to calling "Shaolin," shaped the group's imagination. "I look at us like King Kong," he said. "Being on an island, with breathing space, is what allowed us to grow to our full capacity." RZA recalled how he and his cousins always rode the lower level of the ferry, where hustlers sold loose cigarettes and joints, to watch the films—notably *Shaolin* and *Wu Tang* and *Five Deadly Venoms*—that inspired their argot and tags. Or most of them, anyway. If the "Wu name" of the Clan's unofficial tenth member, Cappadonna, wasn't at least partly inspired by the name of the local priest-cum-war-hero honored here on Father Capodanno Boulevard (named for local son Vincent Capodanno, who died in Vietnam giving last rites to fallen soldiers there) then I'll eat my hoodie. Which is all part of why it felt extra-special when in 2019 Wu-Tang's home borough got not merely a street named for the group but an entire district. The city's official sign for the Wu-Tang District hangs on a block whose storefronts appeared in the group's first music video and which was more recently in the news as the place where a man who hustled a living selling loose cigarettes there, Eric Garner, was killed by police who ignored his pleas about being unable to breathe.

The feeling of being under pressure, if not of literal suffocation, is a feeling New Yorkers know—and one whose excess has expressed itself too often, down the decades, in violence involving its citizens and cops. Most such incidents to be turned into place-names, until recently, have recalled safety officers killed at work. The most upsetting pair of these are two of the most recent: In Brooklyn, Detective Rafael L. Ramos Way and Wenjian Liu Way, respectively, honor two officers who were sitting in their patrol car when an unwell gunman, apparently exercised by the spate of killings like Eric Garner's that sparked the Black Lives Matter movement, slayed them in cold blood. But such sites have also been joined by streets recalling civilians whose lives have been taken, in varied ways, by the racist iniquities of our system of policing and prisons. Since 2001, the Soundview section of the Bronx has had a block named for an immigrant from Mali, Amadou Diallo, whose wallet police mistook for a gun before they shot forty-one bullets at him. The corner of East 181st and Prospect, across the borough, has since 2017 been called Kalief Browder Way in honor of a young man whose death by his own hand, after he spent three years in Rikers Island for stealing a backpack, was a key factor in the city deciding to move toward closing its infernal jail.

Such horror stories, and the feeling of being pushed toward the margins of the city's life if not of its subway platforms, animates such essential entries in the New York songbook as the hip-hop classic from 1982 in which Grandmaster Flash and the Furious Five rapped about trying not to lose their heads: "Don't push me / 'cause I'm close to the edge." Other odes to city life, in this town that's never been able to stop thinking or singing about itself, are more celebratory. The most popular and thus the most tiresome of these (at least until Jay-Z and Alicia Keys's "Empire State of Mind" came along) has long been Frank Sinatra's version of the theme song, first sung by Liza Minnelli, to Martin Scorsese's forgettable 1977 film *New York, New York*. That distinction hasn't won Ol' Blue Eyes a New York street (he's got them in Hoboken, his hometown, and in Las Vegas). But the city he hymned is now soaked with street names honoring the makers of its modern soundtrack. While walking home from that new Sesame Street sign by Lincoln Center, I passed corners named, on the Upper West Side, for Leonard Bernstein, Miles Davis, and Duke Ellington. Across the park from where the Duke made his home on 106th Street, in what was once known as El Barrio, you'll find streets named for the great *timbalero* Tito Puente and as-great pianist Charlie Palmieri. Venture higher into Harlem and toward blocks there named for Billie Holiday and for James Brown, and you'll find, on 126th just east of Fifth, a street sign bearing the cumbersome phrase "Art Kane: Harlem 1958 Place." It's where the photographer Art Kane gathered fifty-seven leading figures in jazz around one of that block's stoops, to take a picture for *Esquire* magazine that became the subject, decades later, of the popular documentary film *A Great Day in Harlem*.

It was a great day in Brooklyn Heights, at least for fans of the Beastie Boys, when the childhood playground of the late Adam Yauch, better known as the late great Tibet-loving rapper MCA, became Adam Yauch Park in 2013. Brooklyn's honorific geography of music also includes a block in East Flatbush dubbed Bob Marley Boulevard. It doesn't mark a significant site in the reggae legend's life, but it does toast a part of Brooklyn whose bounty of storefronts hawking jerk chicken and Jamaican patties signals its stature as a main drag and meeting place for the hundreds of thousands of Jamaicans who have in recent decades settled nearby. One of them was a preschool teacher named Voletta Wallace, who had a son who grew up to become perhaps Brooklyn's best-loved music maker of all. Christopher Wallace, the beloved rapper who was known as the Notorious B.I.G. and was martyred by a dumb beef back in 1997, had his memory inscribed for all time on the streetscape of Clinton Hill in 2019, in the form of Christopher "Notorious B.I.G." Wallace Way.

. . .

NOW THAT HIP-HOP IS nearly fifty years old and has joined jazz as a classical music of New York, many neighborhoods have gained street signs hailing its greats. In Queens, the street name honoring Louis Armstrong's longtime home in Corona has been joined, in Hollis, by Run DMC JMJ Way (it's named for the home block of Reverend Run and Jam Master Jay). South of there in St. Albans, whose tonier blocks were once home to jazz luminaries including Ella Fitzgerald, Count Basie, and Lena Horne, there's now a street hailing the late great emotional core of another indispensable nineties hip-hop troupe, A Tribe Called Quest. The corner of Linden Boulevard and 192nd was co-named, after its honoree's sad passing from complications related to diabetes in 2016, as Malik "Phife Dawg" Taylor Way.

Less associated with city life than with rhymes like Phife's or the spotlit lullabies of Broadway is the admixture of rural-tinged Americana and oblique or lefty lyrics that's been known, since the 1950s, as "folk music." But that cultural idiom has always been animated by urbane hipsters' nostalgia for an imagined rural past, and its growth was in key ways fostered by New York. It was in coffee spots of the Village, of course, that the Weavers and then Bob Dylan got their starts, and Dylan's charismatic if less famous comrade Dave Van Ronk, whose memoir inspired the Coen brothers' movie *Inside Llewyn*

Davis, now has a street there. In Staten Island, a street called Stanley Jay Way honors the co-proprietor of a destination emporium of stringed instruments, Mandolin Brothers, where many folkies got theirs and which Joni Mitchell invoked in that tune you may recall from *Hejira* ("I went to Staten Island, Sharon / to buy a mandolin"). And now Coney Island's got a street named for the Okie granddaddy of them all. Woody Guthrie spent much of the 1940s in Brooklyn with his family, in an apartment just down Mermaid Avenue from where Nathan and Ida Handwerker Way hails the birthplace of Nathan's Famous Hot Dogs. As of 2019, Woody Guthrie Way marks where its honoree was living when he first recorded "This Land Is Your Land" and wrote countless other ditties, too, including one about the venal racism of a prominent local landlord named Fred Trump.

Fred Trump's venal and racist son, as the world now knows, made his way from Queens to Manhattan before leveraging his career in real estate to launch one on TV. The trajectory of Donald Trump's life mirrors a most common New York tale—the young upstart from the outer boroughs making her or his way to Manhattan to take on the world—that's also audible in the musical output of Queens' most musical high school. Among the alumni of Forest Hills High School who've made the journey across the Queensboro Bridge to "the city" are Burt Bacharach, Paul Simon and Art Garfunkel (whose "59th Street Bridge Song" was all about feeling groovy while doing so), and a crew of more punkish white boys from the class of 1974. Those boys, the Ramones, recently gained the unique distinction of having streets co-named in their honor both where they came of age and where they grew up. Joey Ramone Place in the East Village was joined, in 2016, by The Ramones Way outside their alma mater. But if Queens gave the world both punk rock and "Parsley, Sage, Rosemary and Thyme," it's the Bronx that has most shaped the sonic culture of the world in recent decades—and which now has a bevy of honorary streets reflecting how.

For in addition to those signs hailing the doo-wop that seemed to grow from its sidewalks after the war, and a slew of jazz titans recently added to its corners by the Bronx Music Heritage Center, the Boogie Down borough has in recent years begun to tout the all-American sounds forged here, too, by immigrants from the Caribbean. Hip Hop Boulevard, otherwise known as a section of Sedgwick Avenue by the Harlem River, marks where, in the community room of a NYCHA-run building here in 1973, a Jamaican kid who called himself Herc and who loved spinning records and talk-singing over their instrumental breaks, hosted what's recalled as "the first hip-hop party." The complex of music and culture that grew from the ashes of the ensuing years, during which the Bronx was nearly burned to the ground by poverty and its own insurance-seeking landlords, would go on to conquer New York and then the world, thanks to figures like another early hip-hop hero—DJ Scott La Rock of Boogie Down Productions—who's now recalled by a street, DJ Scott La Rock Boulevard, in Kingsbridge. Two elements of hip-hop culture that were vitally evolved by kids of Puerto Rican parentage—graffiti-writing and breakdancing—haven't yet been honored by streets. But there are many that honor another new music, birthed in those years and a little earlier, by those young Nuyoricans' uncles and cousins. That music, lending old Cuban rhythms a brash new timbre with Bronx trombones, came to be marketed as "salsa" and to rule, for a time, Latinx radio and dance floors across the hemisphere.

Among that music's most vital wellsprings was a record store that has guarded the corner of Prospect and Longwood in the South Bronx since 1941: It is called Casa Amadeo, its longtime proprietor is hailed there in the name of Miguel Ángel (Mike) Amadeo Way. Nearby streets honor Arsenio Rodríguez, the Cuban composer whose LPs Mike Amadeo sold by the bushel and whose mastery of Cuban *son* gave salsa its beat, as well as two potent singers—Puerto Rico–born Héctor Lavoe and Cuba-born Celia Cruz—pushed to salsa's fore by executives at Fania Records, the company responsible for turning salsa into a thing. Far be it for the Bronx, though, to leave its Latin music heritage to official canon makers: There's also a block here named for the Afro-Cuban singer who was never a performer slick enough to be pushed on the world by Fania's marketers, but who's still recalled, by the music's leading lights and lovers, as the Queen of Latin Soul: To find La Lupe Way, you get off the 6 train by the Bronx Tow Pound and walk over to East 140th Street.

Nowadays, Spanish-language radio here is dominated by Dominican bachata and by reggaeton, but the borough's most talented exponent of hip-hop music in the 1990s was Puerto Rican, too. Raised Christopher Rios in Longwood, he named himself Big Punisher and grew beloved as Big Pun before he died of complications from obesity in 2000. Around the corner from Casa Amadeo, there's a mural to his memory that's become a pilgrimage site for Big Pun's fans. But he doesn't have a street named after him—yet. And the same's true of the most famous Bronxite of all: the dancer turned actor turned ageless pop personage known as J.Lo, who made a biopic of Héctor Lavoe, with her ex Marc Anthony, named *El Cantante* (The Singer) for Lavoe's most famous song. Jennifer Lopez has always insisted, no matter how her star's risen and which leading man she's dating in Manhattan or Miami, on still being "Jenny from the block." One doesn't doubt that decades from now, the block she grew up on, in Castle Hill, will be dubbed Jennifer Lopez Way. Such is her stardom's brightness and staying power that one is almost surprised that hasn't happened already. But I may have gained a clue into why it hasn't when one day I took the 6 train to Castle Hill and found her childhood home, on a block that dead-ends into the Cross Bronx Expressway and is lined with more fences than trees. From a stoop across the street, an old man in a Yankees hat confirmed that the modest triple-decker I stood before was indeed the place where David Lopez and his wife, Guadalupe, raised their girls, but that, no—he spoke with the authority of a dude who'd been there forever—he hadn't seen Jenny on the block in a long time.

8.

MAKING PLACE:
NAMES OF THE FUTURE

In Jackson Heights is a corner sign that's easy not to notice if you're rushing past but whose letters are each assigned a worth in points via subscript numbers, as on a row of Scrabble tiles: $35T_1H_4$ $A_1V_4E_1N_1U_1E_1$. There, amid the handsome six-story apartment houses of what's now the Jackson Heights Historic District, this sign shares a corner with the neighborhood's Community Methodist Church. It was in the church's basement that an architect named Alfred Mosher Butts perfected a board game he invented, which he called Criss Cross Words, by playing it here with his neighbors during the Depression. (Its name was changed when he sold it to a manufacturer in Connecticut who marketed it as Scrabble.) A version of the $35T_1H_4$ $A_1V_4E_1N_1U_1E_1$ sign first appeared here in the 1990s—it was installed by a guerrilla urbanist with a sense of history but without city permission. Its subtlety perhaps helped that unofficial sign remain in place for about a dozen years—long enough for it to become a neighborhood landmark. Which is why, after it was finally removed by the Department of Transportation, the area's new City Council member made its restoration an issue in his campaign for office and, in 2011, the Scrabble corner became official.

This marker of the birthplace of the world's most popular word game (Scrabble's physical version has sold some 150 million copies; its digital version helps millions more fill their idle hours) is its own win for highlighting some of the lesser-known heroes and histories of the urban landscape. But that's not all that resonates about the sign's aspect and site. When Alfred Mosher Butts moved into his apartment across the street from the church, Jackson Heights' six-story buildings were new: The Queensboro Corporation had built them to welcome the opening of what's now the 7 train to Manhattan—and the only-white tenants they enticed to move into them. Over the decades since, the handsome bricks-and-trees appearance of the area's streets hasn't changed much. But who fills them up has. A clue as to how is glimpsed on a sign outside Community Methodist: Whereas in Butts's day, the church was an Anglophone congregation, it now offers weekly services in Mandarin, Spanish, Korean, and Bahasa Indonesian. And that's but a tiny sample of the tongues spoken on nearby streets and in apartment houses whose tenant directories, lists of many-splendored surnames, read like a roll call at the UN.

Nowadays, fully four of every ten local laws passed

by the City Council involve adding new honorary names
to New York's streets—in 2019, they approved putting up
no fewer than 184 signs to mark them (and authorized
corrections to 25 more from recent years that contained
errors). Some New Yorkers think it's a bit much. Among
them may be the one who has done us all the favor of
keeping track of these signs, Gilbert Tauber. "There are
about twelve thousand total intersections in the city," he
told me one afternoon. "But they're going fast. You might
say that in matters of naming, we've grown promiscuous."

We were sitting in Tauber's favorite diner on the
Upper West Side. It was a few days before his go-to spot
for apple pie, along with every other eatery in this city,
would close because of a novel coronavirus that also
halted the City Council's business. I'd been consulting Tauber's wonderful website for years, but never met
him. When I emailed him to meet, he told me to come
to the Metro Diner and "look for an old guy in a fedora."
The spry octogenarian I found by doing so doffed his
hat as I joined him in a booth near the corner of 103rd
and Broadway—Humphrey Bogart Place. When I men-
tioned where my toddler attended preschool, he asked if
I knew that the mansion turned yeshiva on its block was
built by the same Gilded Age magnate of electricity, Isaac
L. Rice, in whose honor Ohm and Watt Streets were
named in the Bronx. And then he told me, over a slice of
his favorite dessert, how his fascination with names was
sparked, during his own Bronx boyhood, when a street

he'd known his whole life as Boscobel Avenue ("We pronounced it Boss-KO-bull") was changed overnight, in 1944, to Edward L. Grant Avenue. Neither Tauber's parents nor anyone else could tell him who Edward L. Grant was—an experience he credits with sowing his devotion, later on, to the Municipal Reference Library near City Hall. He has spent large chunks of his retirement parsing the library's records to produce concise annotations for every street name change in city history, first for his own edification and then for sharing on that wonderful website, Oldstreets.com—where you can now learn that Edward L. Grant was the first Major League baseball player to be killed in World War I.

Tauber moved down to the Village after leaving the Army and fed his yen for city history in the 1950s by taking and then helping lead walking tours of lower Manhattan organized by the Municipal Art Society and also by the group, Friends of Cast Iron Architecture, that saved SoHo's old buildings from the wrecking ball. In the run-up to the 1964 World's Fair, he worked for the New York Convention and Visitors Bureau, producing guidebooks for an organization which, in the 1970s, revived "the Big Apple," an old nickname for the city that was first popularized, as you can learn from Oldstreets .com, by a jazz-age turf writer for the *Morning Telegraph* named John J. Fitz Gerald. (Fitz Gerald's coinage is now commemorated in a sign for the Big Apple Corner, natch, by where he lived on 54th Street.) Tauber then spent most of his career as an urban planner, working for varied city and state agencies. Like many in that field devoted to shaping the city's future, he never let go of his fascination with the occluded past of streets whose names once graced city maps but don't anymore. He became a maven of the archives containing information on those streets, and gained a more comprehensive knowledge of them than anyone alive. He became "our go-to streets guy." And part of the reason he agreed to extend his connoisseurship of the city's old street names to its new honorary ones, when Manhattan's borough historian asked him to do so, was because he thought Local Law 28 would be a great help to his friends whose job it was to update the official city map, which is still kept on giant sheets of mylar, with every name change or cockamamie honorific. "Do you know," he asked, "how hard it used to be for those guys to change a name on the map, or fit in a new one?"

Tauber also had concerns, though, about what the new system had wrought. "I still think of street names like public utilities," he said. "They're there to help people get from one to the other. Which is why people don't like it when you fiddle with them too much. I do think, even with honorary names, there should be limits." He had specific ones in mind. "In the Bronx, they gave a street to Regis Philbin by where he grew up to mark, I think, his thirtieth year in show business. Nothing against Regis, but I think you should be dead before you get a street named after you." In this, Tauber reminded me of an old caution: Thomas Jefferson, who decried "the mania of giving names . . . after persons still living," arguing that "death alone can seal the title of any man to this honor, by putting it out of his power to forfeit it." Death, Jefferson argued, marks an end to shifts in one's reputation. (But, as contemporary views of the man who presided over Monticello have shown, time can have a way of shifting one's standing.) Tauber's worry was that the Council members' current practice of awarding honorary streets was more about appeasing certain constituents than about making all of their lives better. But he also plainly loved these street names. When I asked him if he had a favorite, he looked like I'd asked him to choose a favorite child. I pressed. He allowed that the corner of 35th Avenue and 81st Street, out in Queens near LaGuardia Airport, was extra-dear.

I knew what he meant. "The Scrabble Corner?"

"The Scrabble Corner."

MY FRIEND SUKETU, WHO grew up a couple blocks from the Scrabble Corner, likes to talk about his Gujarati parents' surprise when they moved here in the seventies from India. They marveled then at how people who back in Mumbai had been at each other's throats—Hindus and Muslims, children of Bangladesh and Bangalore—now shared buildings and streets in a land whose rule of law

and promise of a better life allowed them to bury ancestral grudges (at least when not behind their apartments'
closed doors). Suketu and his Indian friends called their
neighborhood Jaikisan Heights. Their Colombian neighbors called it Chapinero, along a stretch of 37th Avenue
that's lined with the same purveyors of cheesy buñuelos
and passionfruit cholados you'll find in a desirable district
of the same name in Bogotá. The Indians and Colombi-
ans and Bangladeshis are all still here. But now they've
also been joined by Hondurans and Afghanis and Tibet-
ans and speakers of Mexico's indigenous languages from
Oaxaca and Nayarit. Each group has its own nicknames
for this part of Queens that's grown famous to demogra-
phers for its density and diversity of the kind of people—
immigrants—who know better than anyone the power of
names to register both possibility and limitation, obstacles
and aspiration.

The few square miles around the church where Scrabble was invented are home to speakers of more languages
than any comparably sized piece of the world's skin. In
New York today, according to the Census, some two hundred tongues are spoken. The real number, according to
my linguist friends at the Endangered Language Alliance, is at least eight hundred and perhaps many more—a
number that makes New York City in the first decades
of the twenty-first century not merely the most linguistically diverse city in world history, but the most
linguistically diverse city that will ever exist. Over the

past several millennia, linguists say, human beings have communicated with each other in tens of thousands of tongues, but are now down to some seven thousand—and losing more by the week. What dies with the last speakers of endangered languages from the Himalayas or the Americas' first nations or Italy's old regions, whose discrete dialects have been subsumed under "standard Italian," aren't just words—gone, too, are entire histories and mythologies and ways of describing life on earth. But it's a remarkable fact of New York's current ethnic mix that many of those endangered languages are kept alive by those driving cabs or busing tables in the city now. Words birthed to describe Bhutan's peaks or the forests of Guatemala are being used today to describe the concrete jungles of New York. And nowhere is the density of such tongues more palpable—or audible on the streets—than in this stretch of north-central Queens where Suketu and I like to meet up for Salvadoran pupusas, or parathas from his homeland, with Ross or Daniel from the Endangered Language Alliance and members of their marvelous network—speakers of Quechua and Garifuna and the ǂʼAmkoe tongue, from Botswana, that sounds like kissing. If we're lucky, Suketu will treat us all to a few words from one of the tongues that all this mixing has birthed in New York: the Gujarati-Yiddish pidgin that his family of diamond merchants, engaged in a business long dominated here by Jewish Hasidim, employed to haggle over jewels.

The story of what transformed this once-white enclave

into a world-historical Babel of people and languages, and a marvelous microcosm of polyglot New York now, is a story in part about two key pieces of legislation from the Civil Rights era that transformed the United States. One is the Immigration and Nationality Act of 1965, which ended old limits on immigration from the world's "darker nations," and the other is the Fair Housing Act of 1968, which made discrimination in housing against minorities, including those new arrivals, illegal. The combined result was a tide of new people from a number of world regions entering the housing market—South Asia, the Caribbean, West Africa, South America, and the Middle East—who were previously underrepresented in New York's ethnic mix. With them came new patterns of residence that transformed the names that fill its neighborhoods.

Since 2004 in lower Manhattan, a piece of Allen Street running between Chinatown and where the Lower East Side once served as a famous landing place for new arrivals from Europe's impoverished fringe has borne the official co-name Avenue of the Immigrants. Today that part of the Lower East Side is a landing place less for immigrants than for NYU grads with trust funds and faux-bohemian bankers. The Avenue of the Immigrants would perhaps be a more appropriate tag for any number of thoroughfares—Roosevelt Avenue in Queens, 149th Street in the Bronx, Neptune Avenue in post-Soviet southern Brooklyn—that now serve as vital hubs for new arrivals to a city whose foreign-born residents and their kids now compose a third of the city's populace, the same proportion as at Ellis Island's peak. The "new immigration" shares much with the old. But among its distinctions are the ways that today's "transnational" immigrants have been able—with the help of the Internet, cheap airfare, and money-wiring services whose outlets occupy what seem like every other storefront on such immigrant thoroughfares—to maintain strong ties to home nations for which remittances are a lifeblood. Another is the lack of pressure they feel, unlike the European immigrants who once flocked to New York's docks, to dive headlong into a melting pot whose end effect and goal, for the Germans and Irish and others who embraced its heat in the nineteenth century, was to shed their foreign identities and accents to become American by becoming, in a word, generically white.

Such groups' success in doing so is registered by the many street and neighborhood names that once marked their enclaves but are now long gone. The successful assimilation of New York's once highly visible populace of ethnic Germans into the undifferentiated mass of American whiteness was marked not merely by the transformation of, say, Drumpfs into Trumps, but also by the disappearance from New York's map of Rhinelanders' Row, Rhinelanders' Alley, and Rhinelanders' Wharf. For other historic groups whose climb to whiteness took longer, such name changes were even more common. There's a reason that I have cousins, on my family's Schapiro side, who became Shephards to get ahead in business: It's the same reason there are countless Jews here named Green and Edwards whose forebears were Greenbergs and Epsteins, who perhaps lived, when there were such places in lower Manhattan, on Jew Street or Jews Alley.

Manhattan's Chinatown is home not merely to restaurants owned by the old immigrants' heirs who've moved to the 'burbs, as in nearby Little Italy, but also to the kinds of businesses—banks, hair salons, funeral parlors—that indicate its status as a living destination for new arrivals from Guangdong and Fuzhou. Since the first Cantonese laundries and boardinghouses opened on Mott and Bayard Streets in the 1870s, the old Dutch and English names of nearby blocks have grown steeped in Chinese lore: the curving block of Doyers Street, once home to America's first Chinese-language theater, became known as Bloody Angle, thanks to its popularity as a place for local tongs' "hatchet men" to ambush rivals. From that day to this, the area's residents have never seemed too concerned with changing its public nomenclature or trumpeting to outsiders the fact that, say, the lingua franca of the neighborhood's East Broadway corridor now isn't Cantonese but Fujian. The same is true of Mandarin speakers from China's north and west who've also traversed the Golden Door to establish swelling new Chinatowns in Flushing, Queens, and along the N train's route across southwest Brooklyn from Sunset Park into the bit of Bay Ridge that was once Norwegian-tinged but is now dominated by daughters and sons of Fuzhou. Part of the reason they call their enclave there "Eighth Avenue" has to do with the numbered name of its main shopping drag. Another is to do with the number eight's association, in their culture, with luck.

There are doubtless hundreds of such place-words here that were coined by language speakers much less numerous than China's to riff on their own tongues' words for "luck" or "peril" or "hope," or to describe new homes for themselves or far-off kin. Most such instances of place-making-through-naming never become official, or are even unknown to non-speakers. Many others become vital neighborhood landmarks, not marked by any sign but known to all: Every habitué of South Harlem will tell you that 116th Street between Lenox (aka Malcolm X) and Frederick Douglass is Little Senegal. There are new arrivals to the city, notably those not carrying papers or who've come as refugees, for whom proclaiming their presence is a danger. But where some older enclaves had names born more of others' prejudice than their own pride, there's a marked trend now to turn their presence into a name on a street (or several).

Where Manhattan has its official Little Brazil, Queens now boasts a Tibet Place and Calle Colombia. If a driven group of petitioners get their way in Woodside, it may soon have a Little Manila, too. The Bronx has a sign, over a stretch of Starling Avenue dominated by

Bangladeshis, stating its name as Bangla Bazaar. In 2017, both that borough and Brooklyn gained streets that signal both boroughs' boom in populace from Mexico: They're called Cinco de Mayo Way, in honor not of the holiday on which patrons of Mexican restaurants love to drink, but of a famous nineteenth-century battle in the Mexican city—Puebla—from whence many of New York's Mexican immigrants hail. The City Councilman who fought to make the Scrabble Corner official, Danny Dromm, is a pink-skinned holdover from the area's past who loves its present ("Why *shouldn't* a gay Irishman represent America's most diverse neighborhood?"); he has sponsored other honorary names there, including Mount Everest Way, which hails its Nepalis, and Diversity Plaza, down by the subway stop where *Desi*-dominated 73rd Street meets the Ecuadoran-owned check-cashing joints of Roosevelt Avenue. Many members of the city's new ethnic communities, it seems plain, have come to feel like Haitian American state assemblywoman Rodneyse Bichotte, who saw her years-long quest to have part of Flatbush renamed Little Haiti come to fruition after Donald Trump called her homeland a "shithole": "We thought it was time to claim our territory," Bichotte said, "and let people see who we are." (The only parallel municipal honor is gaining an annual parade.) Others have availed themselves, in the hunt for recognition, of more digital modes of place-making. In the Morris Park area of the Bronx that boasts that street named for Regis Philbin, a Yemeni control

supervisor at JFK airport named Yahay Obeid success-
fully petitioned Google Maps to splash a large label over
the blocks where Mr. Philbin played as a boy and where
the children of Obeid and a critical mass of other Yemenis
do now. It reads, in Google's all-caps font, "LITTLE
YEMEN."

Such quests for recognition, by immigrants and
others on the city's margins who've used the power of
names to make its streets home, are allied to other trends
in a city whose dominant culture and norms keep shifting. Once upon a time, New York's abundant Jews hid
their heritage. Now the city's mayor is dogged by accusa-
tions of having changed his original German name (he
was born Warren Wilhelm before becoming Bill de Blasio) to appeal to Jewish voters. And many immigrants are
rejecting altogether the need felt by their forebears to fit
in. The novelist Viet Thanh Nguyen, in one of the *New
York Times'* most read op-eds from recent years, titled
"America, Say My Name," describes his experience as an
immigrant kid trying to do so by calling himself "Joey"
and "Troy"—and his determination, now, that his fellow Americans call him by his true name. Nguyen's essay
also included riffs on a student whose name was Yaseen
but who wished it wasn't, and on Nguyen's own decision
to name his own son Ellison, after the author of *Invisible Man.* He concluded it thus: "Yaseen. Ellison. Viet.
Nguyen. All American names, if we want them to be. All

of them a reminder that we change these United States of America one name at a time."

That we do. And the reminder only seems to gain urgency as people here and everywhere, during the presidency of a New Yorker openly hostile to their aims, grow increasingly keen to confront names and monuments that honor figures or values that don't match evolved modern mores. And many are determined not merely to see such markers removed from the public square, but also to erect new ones that make underknown histories and figures newly visible in public life.

THIS MOVEMENT BEGAN DOWN SOUTH with the removal, at first halting and then more frequent and now de rigueur, of statues of old Confederates. But it's also been active in New York. A commission appointed by the mayor to identify "symbols of hate" on city property unanimously approved a call to remove from Fifth Avenue a monument to J. Marion Sims, a "father of gynecology" who honed his craft by operating on enslaved women without anesthesia or their consent. In the Manhattan Beach area of Brooklyn, residents campaigned for years to change the name of Corbin Place, which was named in honor of Austin Corbin, a Brooklyn potentate who in the late 1800s built up the neighborhood but also headed up the American Society for the Suppression of

Jews. They came up with an inspired solution: They got a local law passed that left the place's name intact but officially changed its honoree to a woman of the same surname, Margaret Corbin, whose claim to fame was her valor as the foremost woman participant in the American Revolutionary War.

Margaret Corbin wasn't one of the three hundred women that Rebecca Solnit and I included, in 2016, on a reimagining of the city's iconic subway map with each of its stops renamed for an illustrious woman who made a mark on or grew up in their vicinity. One of our aims with "City of Women," as we called that map, was to make a point about the extent to which in New York, as in every city I've ever been to, ninety-nine percent of everything is named for or honors the achievements or legacies of men. In highlighting the achievements and sheer number of mighty women who've shaped New York (and simply getting a kick out of imagining boarding the subway at a stop called Jane Jacobs, transferring at one called Grace Jones, and getting off at the one named Yoko Ono), we wanted to pose the question of how people, and young women in particular, might carry themselves differently in a city that honored their gender. But as the map grew popular and came to be displayed on screens across the city, with the MTA's blessing and at a time when the Me Too movement and women's marches were fostering a larger conversation about gender and public space, it caught something of the zeitgeist in a city that has finally begun, with its She Built NYC initiative and otherwise, to build statues not just of imaginary women but real ones.

All these developments felt significant at the time, and remain so. But they've come to look like forerunners of a larger reckoning sparked by a chain of events that no one could have seen coming. It was set off by a novel coronavirus that laid low all of New York but affected nowhere so badly as the immigrant-rich neighborhoods like the area around Diversity Plaza, which for a time became, as Councilman Danny Dromm put it, the "epicenter of the epicenter" of a global emergency.

During a harrowing April when cases and deaths continued to climb, names gained new meanings. While Queens' Elmhurst Hospital became "the epicenter of the epicenter's" medical frontline, the Nom Wah Tea Parlor, located on Chinatown's old Bloody Angle, stayed afloat amid a new Sinophobia by freezing boxes of its dumplings for quarantined patrons. Before the crisis, Governor Andrew Cuomo was known mostly as a brusque and corrupt Albany operator. Now he became, on the strength of his daily press conferences about microbes and ventilators, an unlikely figure of adoration. But that's neither the most notable nor the most surprising aspect of how the city's course was shaped by the stormy spring of 2020. For as the first wave of the crisis waned and the city's people emerged from their apartments with the warming weather, they filled its streets not to rejoice at the virus's vanquishing—not least because it wasn't yet vanquished—but to protest.

"Say their names!" This was the chant that echoed from Harlem, to Union Square, to the expanse of concrete outside the Barclays Center in Brooklyn. "Say their names!" was shouted from megaphones and by masked marchers who clogged the Brooklyn Bridge and stopped traffic on the FDR. "Say their names!" rang outside the Stonewall Inn, cradle of gay liberation. To this call, the responses came in unison:

"Breonna Taylor!" ("Breonna Taylor!")

"Michael Brown!" ("Michael Brown!")

"Sandra Bland!" ("Sandra Bland!")

There were more.

"Sean Bell!" ("Sean Bell!")

"Eric Garner!" ("Eric Garner!")

"Trayvon Martin!" ("Trayvon Martin!")

"Ahmaud Arbery!" ("Ahmaud Arbery!")

"Tamir Rice!" ("Tamir Rice!")

There was one name that sounded most: "George Floyd!"

That Memorial Day, a gruesome video had begun to ricochet around the Internet. Beamed onto the laptops and phone screens of an enervated public, it depicted a murder: the killing, by a uniformed officer of the state, of an unarmed man. George Floyd was Black. His murderer was white. His final plea—"I can't breathe"—matched the last words of New York's own foremost victim of racist policing from recent years, Eric Garner. This phrase was now stenciled on the face masks of citizens who were fighting against a deadly microbe but who now were also fighting a disease not biological but social—the scourge of systemic racism—with a gusto America hadn't seen in decades. The simple slogan around which their movement cohered, "Black Lives Matter," wasn't new: It had circulated on social media and been hoisted aloft during protests by mostly Black youth across the country for years. But now it became, thanks to widespread revulsion at George Floyd's killing and in a nation whose entrenched inequalities were being rubbed brutally raw by COVID-19, a national movement, based in names, that wouldn't be denied.

When in Washington, D.C., Donald Trump responded to the marchers' anguish not with empathy but with scorn, and then cleared a public square with tear gas so he could pose for a photo, Washington's mayor responded by giving that square a new official name— Black Lives Matter Plaza. This inspired Mayor Bill de Blasio to have the slogan painted in giant yellow letters on Fifth Avenue outside Trump Tower. (A campaign with similar but subtler aims, to have the block named Barack Obama Way, would have to wait.) Cities across the country were engulfed in a uniquely American form of unrest—the "race riot"—made new by the fact that these rebellions included as many white participants as Black

ones. From Chicago to L.A. to Louisville and Atlanta—
and from Copenhagen to Sydney to Kingston and Nai-
robi, too—the same exhortation sounded: "Say Their
Names!"

As I walked through Harlem that June, to attend
the dedication of its own Black Lives Matter mural up on
Adam Clayton Powell above 125th Street, the examples I
passed of how and why names can be made to speak were
many. On 116th, I passed Amy Ruth's, where to order off
the menu is to decide among dishes named for Ruby Dee
(fried or baked catfish), Michelle Obama (fried whiting),
or Al Sharpton (chicken and waffles). On 117th, a mural
on a school named for Sojourner Truth depicts luminaries
like her along with images of nearby street signs (Harriet
Tubman, Malcolm X) that were themselves characters of
a kind in the mural's tableau of pride. On 125th loomed
the Apollo Theater, itself nothing if not a constellation
of names—of the countless Black stars who once made
theirs on its stage. But now, on the same block where one
of them, James Brown, was sent home in a casket made
from 24-karat gold, the crowd in their Black Lives Matter T-shirts held aloft instead the names of martyrs both
well known and not. In this neighborhood that also has a
mural on 138th Street educating people how to "KNOW
YOUR RIGHTS" when engaged by the cops, many held
high the names of loved ones and friends who lost their
lives years ago to police violence.

Now that America cared, or was at least acting like it

did on its streets and on Twitter, the sidewalk LinkNYC screens that had featured our "City of Women" map a few months before now listed the names of those too-readily-overlooked victims of violence. "Who knows but that, on the lower frequencies, I speak for you?": So asked Ellison's nameless narrator at the end of *Invisible Man*. Now the names of the invisible were being made to speak. When Governor Cuomo signed into law a new statute banning police from using choke holds, his office called it the Say Their Names Act. Whether that piece of legislation will actually change policing, to say nothing of the larger structures of inequality that mean some citizens are policed and some aren't, remains to be seen. But something, to be sure, was stirring in that summer's haze and tumult.

WHEN IN THE FALL of 2019 I traveled to Bristol, England, for a conference on the future of cities, I took part there in a public conversation whose main subject was how that old port town should contend with its many public landmarks that were named, in Victorian days, for a man whose legacy had grown vexing. When in the 1890s Bristol's leaders sought a figure from its past to honor by affixing his name to a new civic center and erecting a statue of him nearby, the salient fact about Edward Colston, a merchant and philanthropist who died in 1721, was his generosity in funding schools and hospitals there. What had come to matter most a century later was that he'd made a fortune as a slave trader. On that panel, we discussed how Bristol's current leaders might reconcile peoples' fond memories of attending dances at Colston Hall or sharing a first kiss by his statue with the urgent need to contextualize his name more deeply, in situ, with a plaque or other materials to help their grandkids engage his legacy. But in a city whose current citizens include many descendants of enslaved Africans brought to England's Caribbean colonies in the seventeenth and eighteenth centuries by the ships of Colston's Royal African Company, that legacy's hurts were raw. And the following June, Bristol's citizens, in the midst of the Black Lives Matter movement around the world, took matters into their own hands. An exulting throng yanked Colston's figure from his plinth and, while holding iPhones aloft to capture the moment for the world, dumped the old slaver into the River Avon.

Nothing beats a statue, or its tearing down, for staging political dramas—or for exemplifying the ways that history, with the help of a mob's moral certitude, is made to move. Days after Mr. Colston was dunked in England, the leaders of the American Museum of Natural History in New York announced that they would remove a discomfiting statue of that institution's own founding patron, whose image since 1939 had lorded over a Native American and African attendant in front of the museum's steps. Protesters decrying Teddy Roosevelt's execrable views on such people—"I don't go so far as to think that the only good Indian is the dead Indian, but I believe nine out of every ten are"—certainly helped the museum make its decision. When in 1992 New York's City Council enacted Local Law 28, many local politicians availed themselves of the chance to erect more public memorials to Christopher Columbus's arrival in the New World five hundred years earlier, though existing ones were hardly lacking. Not thirty years later, statues of Columbus, seen by many less as a hero than as a herald of colonial violence, have begun to come down.

It's become an article of faith among some to say that such moves deny History, or, on the other side, that they represent an unalloyed index of Progress. It's not hard to rebut the floggers of straw men and peddlers of false equivalence who've contended that many recently removed memorials to dead Confederates, for example, are emblems of "history we shouldn't forget." Their position is willful in its ignorance of the fact that most such statues date not from the time of Jefferson Davis but from the early 1900s, generations later: They were erected, during the most vile phase of the Jim Crow era, to champion the continuance and cause of white supremacy. It also shouldn't be hard, for any true friend of historical truth, to voice anything but unalloyed gratitude for a new memorial that rose in Alabama in 2018 to take their place: the National Memorial for Peace and Justice, in Montgomery. It commemorates the thousands of Black Americans who were killed by racial terrorists between the eras of Recon-

struction and Civil Rights, under those Confederate statues' approving gaze. What that memorial in Montgomery
makes plain, along with allied efforts to mark where the
lynchings it recalls occurred, all across the South, is that
sometimes it takes engaged and righteous citizens—in
that case, stirred to action by the remarkable lawyer and
activist Bryan Stevenson—to make our past plain, too.

Names are a subtler form of public memorial than
a statue made of stone: You can't toss a word in the river.
There are reasons to be grateful this is so—but also vital
reasons to engage why, and how best to address objections
to them, too.

A few years ago, Yale University faced a demand
from students and others to remove an offending name
from one of its dorms—a request many other institutions
have contended with since. The dorm was named for
John C. Calhoun, a prominent alum who was also a notorious antebellum statesman, slave owner, and racist. The
first protests against the name were subtle: When I was a
nineteen-year-old living in Calhoun, my lefty friends and
I joked that it was a good thing we lived in the old racist's dorm or else we never would have gotten to meet the
sundry Black eminences who, when invited to campus to
speak on lives and careers devoted to undoing slavery's
legacies, were invariably invited to do so at Calhoun. But
such gestures weren't enough.

The administration ultimately decided to remove
Calhoun's name, in favor of an alumna more in keeping

with its values. The rationale offered was that such name changes should be rare, but Calhoun was an extreme case. More than simply a man of his time, he viewed slavery "not as an evil," as he put it, "but as a good—a positive good." Calhoun, according to one learned contemporary, "changed the state of opinion and the manner of speaking and writing upon this subject." It mattered, in other words, that he was widely recognized in his own day as not merely a defender of slavery but a fierce advocate for it, whose central legacy is as a man whose hateful ideas shaped history.

We have long made distinctions, in building monuments or changing them, between history's chief advocates of cruelty and those who were only compliant followers. Stalingrad was renamed, though it retains many symbols of people who endured or even shaped Stalin's era. There's a reason we don't see squares or gaze at monuments named for Goebbels in Berlin. But one reason historians warn against condescending to the past is to selfishly safeguard our present: Who's to say our great-grandchildren won't reach a consensus that eating dead animals was the height of barbarism, and demand the expunging of all non-vegetarians from their college syllabi and public squares? And there's another, subtler source of danger lurking in such condescension—the lack of credit we give to our own ancestors who may have loathed or been victimized by the "peculiar institution" themselves, but who understood, by attaching new meanings to place-names redolent with it—"Washington," "Jackson," "Jamaica," "Harlem"—that part of the power of names, and of our power over them, is that their meanings can change.

This has implications not merely for the names we get rid of, but also for the ones, we'd do well to recall, that we replace them with. When in the 1970s and '80s the United States gained those hundreds of boulevards honoring Martin Luther King Jr., his name's prominence was both a proud achievement for backers of his radical vision and a testament to his domestication, by public officials who often plunked his name across Black neighborhoods without consulting residents, as a defanged preacher of peace. His namesake streets, which tend to be in those towns' poorest and most segregated areas, have given his moniker new meaning. "To name any street for King," observed the journalist Jonathan Tilove in a book about visiting many of them, "is to invite an accounting of how the street makes good on King's promise or mocks it." Chris Rock was more succinct: "If you're on Martin Luther King Boulevard, there's some violence going down." We can celebrate, in coming years, the many different varieties of humans whose names—female and queer and of-color and differently abled—should continue, by rights, to multiply on our maps. But we'll also do well to recall, as we do, that names can have minds of their own.

· · ·

A NAME, IT MAY BE TRUE, can never be completely divorced from its root. But a name is also an opportunity. And it's a hope—at the least, a hope by its coiner that it will stick: that its destiny will be more akin to, say, the fate of Adam Clayton Powell's namesake avenue in Harlem than that of the official moniker, since 2008, of the Robert F. Kennedy Bridge, which no New Yorker doesn't still call the Triborough. (How do you distinguish if the person describing their drive into Manhattan from Queens or the Bronx is a native or a tourist? Listen for reference to "the Robert F. Kennedy Bridge.") The reason some new names stick and some don't can have less to do with politics than with euphony—than with the way a name strikes our ears or rolls off our tongues or suits a story's beats. But, fundamentally, the reason a name sticks is the image or vision it offers of a place and its people.

"Landscape is history made visible," wrote the geographer J. B. Jackson. In recent years, I've led workshops on maps and mapping in each of New York's boroughs and have seen this truth up close. Asking participants in those workshops to visually represent landscapes both traversed and imagined produces an astonishing range: maps of quiet and of noise; maps of memories and of happiness; maps with made-up names ("Ex-landia": don't go where my ex lives); maps of places where refugees seek sanctuary; maps of the streets where one feels most comfortable on two wheels (as playfully and poignantly represented by a young woman I met who runs an organization called The Brown Bike Girl); maps of the curb cuts and elevators that make urban life possible for those of who are disabled and get around not on two wheels but on four. Each of us, in these ways, inhabits a different city. Each of us, in the names we use to navigate it, also lives in one that is shared.

If landscape is history made visible, the names we call its places are the words we use to forge maps of meaning in the city. On its streets, we make our way to different fates, but also intersect, if sometimes for only a moment, in shared spaces whose names can embody common understanding—and can become the signs under which we learn not merely to see each other but to see through, too, to possible futures.

ACKNOWLEDGMENTS

This project began during my joyous time as the inaugural writer in residence at Pioneer Works in Brooklyn. Deep thanks to Camille Drummond for getting me there; to Gabe Florenz and Janna Levin for making it home; and to Ben Castenon for connecting the dots.

Nothing helps one love place-names, or why they matter to cities, like making maps. The dear collaborators and co-thinkers with whom I got to make the maps that comprise *Nonstop Metropolis* have animated this project, too. Big ups, always, to Rebecca Solnit, Jonathan Tarleton, and Garnette Cadogan. Without what's grown from the "infinite" series of atlases that Rebecca launched years ago, I'm not sure where I'd be.

Gratitude, too, to Ross Perlin and the indomitable Endangered Language Alliance; to Gilbert Tauber, mensch; and to Suketu Mehta, king of Bleecker Street and Jackson Heights alike.

To my agent nonpareil, Zoe Pagnamenta, and to Sarah Larson and everyone at ZPA. To Eric Klinenberg and the Institute for Public Knowledge at NYU. And to Diana Secker Tesdell, whose belief in this book, and the knowledge she brought to it, has been fortifying, indeed. To everyone at Pantheon.

Pablo and Mirissa Neff gave a lot of our Sundays to this book. You two won't, I promise, have to give any more. But here's to sweet memories of Glass Bottle Beach—and to going back soon.

INDEX OF PLACE-NAMES

A NOTE ABOUT THE AUTHOR

Joshua Jelly-Schapiro is a geographer and writer. His work has appeared in *The New Yorker, The New York Review of Books, The New York Times, New York,* and *Harper's Magazine,* among many other publications. He is the author of *Island People: The Caribbean and the World* and cocreator (with Rebecca Solnit) of *Nonstop Metropolis: A New York City Atlas.* He is a scholar-in-residence at the Institute for Public Knowledge at New York University, where he also teaches.

A NOTE ON THE TYPE

This book was set in Granjon, a type named in compliment to Robert Granjon, a type cutter and printer active in Antwerp, Lyons, Rome, and Paris from 1523 to 1590. Granjon, the boldest and most original designer of his time, was one of the first to practice the trade of typefounder apart from that of printer.

Linotype Granjon was designed by George W. Jones, who based his drawings on a face used by Claude Garamond (ca. 1480–1561) in his beautiful French books. Granjon more closely resembles Garamond's own type than do any of the various modern faces that bear his name.

Composed by Digital Composition, Berryville, Virginia
Printed and bound by Friesens Printing, Altona, Canada
Designed by Maria Carella

10-16-21